D0820837

INTRODUCING
ISSUES WITH
OPPOSING
VIEWPOINTS®

College

Jacqueline Langwith, *Book Editor*

GREENHAVEN PRESS
A part of Gale, Cengage Learning

GALE
CENGAGE Learning™

Detroit • New York • San Francisco • New Haven, Conn • Waterville, Maine • London

Christine Nasso, *Publisher*
Elizabeth Des Chenes, *Managing Editor*

© 2009 Greenhaven Press, a part of Gale, Cengage Learning

Gale and Greenhaven Press are registered trademarks used herein under license.

For more information, contact:
Greenhaven Press
27500 Drake Rd.
Farmington Hills, MI 48331-3535
Or you can visit our Internet site at gale.cengage.com

ALL RIGHTS RESERVED.
No part of this work covered by the copyright herein may be reproduced, transmitted, stored, or used in any form or by any means graphic, electronic, or mechanical, including but not limited to photocopying, recording, scanning, digitizing, taping, Web distribution, information networks, or information storage and retrieval systems, except as permitted under Section 107 or 108 of the 1976 United States Copyright Act, without the prior written permission of the publisher.

For product information and technology assistance, contact us at

Gale Customer Support, 1-800-877-4253
For permission to use material from this text or product, submit all requests online at www.cengage.com/permissions

Further permissions questions can be emailed to permissionrequest@cengage.com

Articles in Greenhaven Press anthologies are often edited for length to meet page requirements. In addition, original titles of these works are changed to clearly present the main thesis and to explicitly indicate the author's opinion. Every effort is made to ensure that Greenhaven Press accurately reflects the original intent of the authors. Every effort has been made to trace the owners of copyrighted material.

Cover image © 2009 Jupiterimages.

LIBRARY OF CONGRESS CATALOGING-IN-PUBLICATION DATA

College / Jacqueline Langwith, book editor.
    p. cm. — (Introducing issues with opposing viewpoints)
    Includes bibliographical references and index.
    ISBN 978-0-7377-4336-4 (hardcover)
1. College student orientation—Juvenile literature. 2. Universities and colleges—Admission—Juvenile literature. I. Langwith, Jacqueline.
    LB2343.32.C63 2009
    378.1'98—dc22

                                                                    2008052831

Printed in the United States of America
1 2 3 4 5 6 7 13 12 11 10 09

Contents

Chapter 3: What Factors Impact a Student's Ability to Attend College?

Foreword

Indulging in a wide spectrum of ideas, beliefs, and perspectives is a critical cornerstone of democracy. After all, it is often debates over differences of opinion, such as whether to legalize abortion, how to treat prisoners, or when to enact the death penalty, that shape our society and drive it forward. Such diversity of thought is frequently regarded as the hallmark of a healthy and civilized culture. As the Reverend Clifford Schutjer of the First Congregational Church in Mansfield, Ohio, declared in a 2001 sermon, "Surrounding oneself with only like-minded people, restricting what we listen to or read only to what we find agreeable is irresponsible. Refusing to entertain doubts once we make up our minds is a subtle but deadly form of arrogance." With this advice in mind, Introducing Issues with Opposing Viewpoints books aim to open readers' minds to the critically divergent views that comprise our world's most important debates.

Introducing Issues with Opposing Viewpoints simplifies for students the enormous and often overwhelming mass of material now available via print and electronic media. Collected in every volume is an array of opinions that captures the essence of a particular controversy or topic. Introducing Issues with Opposing Viewpoints books embody the spirit of nineteenth-century journalist Charles A. Dana's axiom: "Fight for your opinions, but do not believe that they contain the whole truth, or the only truth." Absorbing such contrasting opinions teaches students to analyze the strength of an argument and compare it to its opposition. From this process readers can inform and strengthen their own opinions, or be exposed to new information that will change their minds. Introducing Issues with Opposing Viewpoints is a mosaic of different voices. The authors are statesmen, pundits, academics, journalists, corporations, and ordinary people who have felt compelled to share their experiences and ideas in a public forum. Their words have been collected from newspapers, journals, books, speeches, interviews, and the Internet, the fastest growing body of opinionated material in the world.

Introducing Issues with Opposing Viewpoints shares many of the well-known features of its critically acclaimed parent series, Opposing Viewpoints. The articles are presented in a pro/con format, allowing readers to absorb divergent perspectives side by side. Active reading questions preface each viewpoint, requiring the student to approach the material thoughtfully and carefully. Useful charts, graphs, and cartoons supplement each article. A thorough introduction provides readers with crucial background on an issue. An annotated bibliography points the reader toward articles, books, and Web sites that contain additional information on the topic. An appendix of organizations to contact contains a wide variety of charities, nonprofit organizations, political groups, and private enterprises that each hold a position on the issue at hand. Finally, a comprehensive index allows readers to locate content quickly and efficiently.

Introducing Issues with Opposing Viewpoints is also significantly different from Opposing Viewpoints. As the series title implies, its presentation will help introduce students to the concept of opposing viewpoints and learn to use this material to aid in critical writing and debate. The series' four-color, accessible format makes the books attractive and inviting to readers of all levels. In addition, each viewpoint has been carefully edited to maximize a reader's understanding of the content. Short but thorough viewpoints capture the essence of an argument. A substantial, thought-provoking essay question placed at the end of each viewpoint asks the student to further investigate the issues raised in the viewpoint, compare and contrast two authors' arguments, or consider how one might go about forming an opinion on the topic at hand. Each viewpoint contains sidebars that include at-a-glance information and handy statistics. A Facts About section located in the back of the book further supplies students with relevant facts and figures.

Following in the tradition of the Opposing Viewpoints series, Greenhaven Press continues to provide readers with invaluable exposure to the controversial issues that shape our world. As John Stuart Mill once wrote: "The only way in which a human being can make some approach to knowing the whole of a subject is by hearing what can be said about it by persons of every variety of opinion and studying all modes in which it can be looked at by every character of mind. No wise man ever acquired his wisdom in any mode but this." It is to this principle that Introducing Issues with Opposing Viewpoints books are dedicated.

Introduction

"I see the flashing lights of ambulances, and it seems kind of ironic that drinking oneself into alcohol toxicity is how we try to show our independence. When it comes down to it, living on your own is about making decisions—not always the right ones, but, hopefully not so many wrong ones that you lose your chance."

—Natasha Carrie Cohen, "Independence Day," *Chicken Soup for the College Soul*

Samantha Spady, a nineteen-year-old Colorado State University student, died from alcohol poisoning early on the morning of September 5, 2004. As a high school student in Beatrice, Nebraska, Sam—as she was known—was an honor student, a cheerleader, senior class president, and homecoming queen. Her friends and family described her as vibrant, happy, and sweet—an all-American girl. After college, Sam wanted to move west and own a car dealership like her father. In an interview with the *Sioux City* (Nebraska) *Journal*, Sam's mother, Patty, said her daughter chose to go to college at Colorado State University (CSU) because "she wanted to be surrounded by the beauty of the Rocky Mountains." Tragically, Sam never made it beyond the Rocky Mountains nor past her sophomore year at CSU. After having some thirty to forty drinks of beer and vodka in an eleven-hour span, she died of an alcohol overdose alone in a fraternity room on the CSU campus. Many people, including Sam's parents, are trying to educate young college students about binge drinking to prevent what happened to Sam from happening to other young adults. A prominent group of college presidents agrees that educating young people about drinking is a good idea. The group also thinks binge drinking would be lessened if the drinking age were lowered from twenty-one to eighteen. However, many other people think that the current drinking age limit has prevented the deaths of hundreds of young people and lowering it is a bad idea.

Statistics indicate that alcohol and binge drinking—generally defined as having four to five or more drinks in one sittings—are troubling problems for college-aged people. According to the National Institute on Alcohol Abuse and Alcoholism (NIAAA), each year about 1,700 college students between the ages of eighteen and twenty-four die from alcohol-related injuries, many from fatal car accidents. The NIAAA also says that another 599,000 people in this age group are injured, 696,000 are assaulted, and 97,000 are sexually abused—all because of alcohol. According to an Associated Press analysis, 157 college-aged people—including Sam Spady—drank themselves to death from 1999 through 2005.

In 1984 the U.S. government began requiring all states to set twenty-one as the legal drinking age requirement. Since the end of prohibition in the 1930s, most states had set twenty-one as the legal drinking age. However, in the 1970s, at the height of the Vietnam War, many states began lowering the drinking age to eighteen or twenty to more closely align with age limits for enlisting in the military and voting. A few years later, concerns started arising that the lower age limits were increasing traffic fatalities of young people. Around this same time, the awareness of drunk driving increased. The group Mothers Against Drunk Driving (MADD)—formed in 1980—and other organizations began lobbying the federal government to set a national drinking age limit. In 1984, the U.S. Congress responded and enacted the Uniform Drinking Age Act requiring all states to adopt twenty-one as the legal drinking age.

Over one hundred chancellors and college presidents from around the country believe that limiting drinking to those twenty-one or older is leading to a growth of binge drinking on college campuses. In July 2008 a group of college presidents, including the presidents of Dartmouth, Duke, Ohio State, and Syracuse University, formed the Amethyst Initiative—named after an ancient Greek belief that the purple gemstone amethyst could ward off drunkenness. These college presidents believe that setting twenty-one as the drinking age limit has created a culture of dangerous, clandestine binge drinking. They think that telling young people to abstain from alcohol has been ineffective in changing their behavior. The members of the Amethyst Initiative argue that it is illogical and unfair to deem adults under twenty-one as capable of voting, signing contracts, serving on juries, and dying for their country in the military, yet telling them they are not mature enough to have a beer. Furthermore, they believe the drinking age limit of twenty-one forces students to use fake IDs and make ethical compromises that erode their respect for the law.

The Amethyst Initiative was started by John McCardell, the former president of Middlebury College in Vermont. In a 2007 interview with *U.S. News & World Report*, when asked why lowering the drinking age would help prevent binge drinking, McCardell said, "as things stand, alcohol is a reality in the lives of 18-, 19-, and 20-year-olds. And prohibition doesn't work. Public policy should not be to try to change deeply seated human behavior. The goal should be to create the safest possible environment for that reality to take place. . . . If you infantilize people, you can't profess astonishment when you see infantile behavior." McCardell thinks the key to preventing binge drinking is to educate young people about responsible drinking. He thinks modeling alcohol education after drivers' education is a good idea. McCardell and the members of the Amethyst Initiative believe that young people should be educated about alcohol so they can be prepared to deal with alcohol responsibly. They believe that irresponsible drinking is exacerbated by not letting young adults legally drink until they are twenty-one, and they want to have a national debate on the issue.

Many people disagree with the Amethyst Initiative. U.S. Congressman Frank Lautenberg from New Jersey was one of the senators who wrote the 1984 law increasing the drinking age limit. He says that his law saves lives. "Drunk driving needlessly kills thousands of young people every year. That's why I wrote a law to create a national drinking age of 21 and why we fight so hard to reduce drunk driving and save lives on our roads," he said. "This small minority of college administrators wants to undo years of success—that defies common sense. We need to do all we can to protect the national drinking age—a law that saves the lives of drivers, passengers and pedestrians across the country each year." Ronald Ruecker, president of the International Association of Chiefs of Police, agrees. He says that "lowering the minimum drinking age to 18 is both misguided and dangerous. . . . The worst thing any police officer has to do is knock on a door in the dead of night to tell parents that their child will not be coming home because he or she is a victim of impaired driving. Lowering the national drinking age would inevitably lead to more tragedies for more families." Senator Lautenberg and Ronald Reucker are among a group of people who believe that the drinking age limit of twenty-one saves lives by preventing young and immature adults from drinking and driving. They have called on the members of the Amethyst Initiative to reconsider their decision to seek to lower the drinking age.

MADD thinks that part of the problem with binge drinking is the college atmosphere. Alcohol abuse and binge drinking are worse among college-age students in college versus those who are not in college, says MADD. The group believes that college students have easy access to alcohol, and drinking laws are not adequately enforced on college campuses. The solution to college binge drinking, says MADD, involves changing the atmosphere around college campuses and enforcing drinking laws, not changing them.

Sam Spady's mom has not said whether she thinks the drinking age limit should be lowered or not. However, she has much to say on the issue of college binge drinking.

> While college is a wonderful thing, everyone must take responsibility for their own actions. Sam was drinking while she was underaged and she paid a horrible price for those actions. But there is definitely a "drinking to get drunk" mentality on most college campuses. While I don't think there's a way to eliminate all alcohol from every college campus, there must be more education on alcohol's effects.

College requires that young adults make important decisions that can affect their lives in dramatic ways. Many of these decisions are made when the young adult is on the college campus: Should they have a drink at the party even though they are not of legal age? When should they stop drinking? These decisions, though often made in a moment's notice without any forethought, can, as in Sam Spady's case, make the difference between life and death. These decisions should be given as much attention and thought as the decisions young adults make years before the first day of college, such as which college should I attend? How should I pay for college? Can I get into the college of my choice? The contributors to *Introducing Issues with Opposing Viewpoints: College* offer their opinions on many of the important questions young adults must answer about college in the following chapters: "How Should High School Students Prepare for College?" "How Should High School Students Decide Where to Go to College?" and "What Factors Impact a Student's Ability to Attend College?"

Chapter 1

How Should High School Students Prepare for College?

Friends and family attend funeral services for Samantha Spady, who died of alcohol poisoning from binge drinking at Colorado State University.

Everyone Should Go to College

Sandy Baum and Jennifer Ma

"Higher education does pay. It yields a high rate of return for students from all racial/ ethnic groups, for men and for women, and for those from all family backgrounds. It also delivers a high rate of return for society."

In the following viewpoint Sandy Baum and Jennifer Ma contend that college and higher education is beneficial for all individuals and for society. Baum and Ma prepared a report that attempted to quantify the benefits of college. This viewpoint is a summary of the findings from their report. They conclude that the benefits of college include measurable ones, such as that people who attend college earn more money than those who do not. They also found many hard-to-measure benefits of college, such as that college-educated adults are healthier and participate more in their communities. Baum and Ma believe that society needs to do more to ensure that all Americans have access to the benefits of a college education. Baum is a senior policy analyst for the College Board and professor of economics at Skidmore College. Ma is a consultant to the College Board. The College Board, a nonprofit organization, is the developer and administrator of the SAT, PSAT, and AP programs.

Sandy Baum and Jennifer Ma, *Education Pays: The Benefits of Higher Education for Individuals and Society.* New York, NY: College Board, 2007. Copyright © 2007 The College Board. All rights reserved. Reproduced by permission.

  1. Name two nonmonetary benefits to individuals of college that
     Baum and Ma mention.
  2. According to Baum and Ma, despite the progress the United
     States has made in improving educational opportunities, signifi-
     cant differences in higher education participation are still based
     on what kinds of demographic characteristics?
  3. According to Baum and Ma, when the United States is com-
     pared internationally, it ranks higher in overall degree attain-
     ment than it does in the attainment of what kind of degree?

S tudents who attend institutions of higher education obtain a
wide range of personal, financial, and other lifelong benefits;
likewise, taxpayers and society as a whole derive a multitude of
direct and indirect benefits when citizens have access to postsecondary education. Accordingly, uneven rates of participation in higher
education across different segments of U.S. society should be a matter
of urgent interest not only to the individuals directly affected, but
also to public policy makers at the federal, state, and local levels. . . .

The benefits of higher education for individuals and for society as
a whole are both monetary and nonmonetary.

Benefits to Individuals

There is a positive correlation between higher levels of education
and higher earnings for all racial/ethnic groups and for both men
and women.

In addition to earning higher wages, college graduates are more
likely than others to enjoy employer-provided health insurance and
pension benefits.

The income gap between high school graduates and college graduates has increased significantly over time. The earnings benefit is large
enough for the average college graduate to recoup both earnings for-
gone during the college years and the cost of full tuition and fees in
a relatively short period of time.

The considerable nonmonetary rewards of a college education
include better health and greater opportunities for the next generation.

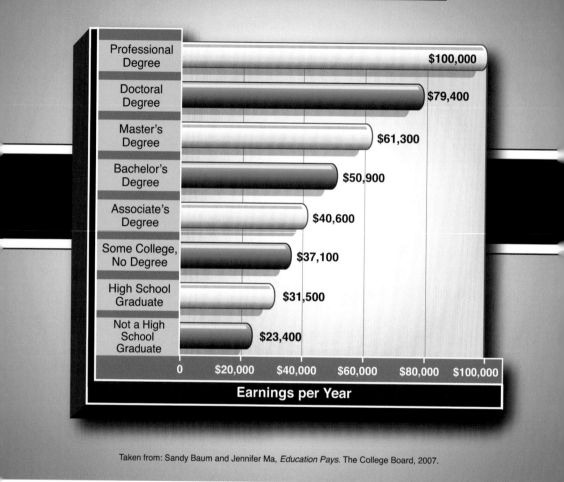

Those with College Degrees Earn More than Those Without, 2005

Degree	Earnings per Year
Professional Degree	$100,000
Doctoral Degree	$79,400
Master's Degree	$61,300
Bachelor's Degree	$50,900
Associate's Degree	$40,600
Some College, No Degree	$37,100
High School Graduate	$31,500
Not a High School Graduate	$23,400

Earnings per Year

Taken from: Sandy Baum and Jennifer Ma, *Education Pays*. The College Board, 2007.

Any college experience produces a measurable return when compared with none, but the benefits of completing a bachelor's degree or higher are particularly large.

Societal Benefits

Higher levels of education correspond to lower unemployment and poverty rates. So, in addition to contributing more to tax revenues than others do, adults with higher levels of education are less likely to depend on social safety-net programs, generating decreased demand on public budgets.

The earnings of workers with lower education levels are positively affected by the presence of college graduates in the workforce.

College graduates have lower smoking rates, more positive perceptions of personal health, and healthier lifestyles than individuals who did not graduate from college.

Higher levels of education are correlated with higher levels of civic participation, including volunteer work, voting, and blood donation, as well as with greater levels of openness to the opinions of others.

Given the extent of higher education's benefits to society, gaps in access to college are matters of great significance to the country as a whole. . . . Despite the progress we have made in improving educational opportunities, participation in higher education differs significantly by family income, parent education level, and other demographic characteristics.

Patterns of Postsecondary Participation

Among students with top test scores, virtually all students from the top quarter of families in terms of income and parental education enroll in postsecondary education, but about 25 percent of those in the lowest socioeconomic quartile do not continue their education after high school.

Differences in family background generate smaller differences in postsecondary participation among students with high test scores than among those with lower levels of measured academic achievement.

Gaps in postsecondary enrollment rates by income and race/ethnicity are persistent. Moreover, black and Hispanic students, as well as low-income students, are less likely than others to complete degrees if they do enroll. Students from rural areas and male students also have relatively lower levels of participation in higher education.

> **FAST FACT**
>
> In 2006, 66 percent of high school students enrolled in college immediately after completing high school, according to the National Center on Education Statistics.

Gaps between individuals who participate and succeed in higher education and those who don't have a major impact on the next

College graduates earn higher wages and are more likely to have employer-provided health insurance and pension benefits than non–college graduates.

generation. The young children of college graduates display higher levels of school readiness indicators than children of parents who did not graduate from college. For high school graduates from families with similar incomes, students whose parents went to college are significantly more likely to go to college themselves than those whose parents did not go to college.

International comparisons indicate that the United States ranks higher in overall degree attainment than in degree attainment in science and engineering.

The story . . . is that higher education does pay. It yields a high rate of return for students from all racial/ethnic groups, for men and for women, and for those from all family backgrounds. It also delivers a high rate of return for society. The specific evidence of these benefits . . . provides the basis for more informed decisions about public and private investments in higher education opportunities.

EVALUATING THE AUTHORS' ARGUMENTS:

In this viewpoint Sandy Baum and Jennifer Ma describe the individual and societal benefits of college. Which benefits that they describe is most important to you? Do you think there are any negatives to attending college? Do you think the authors provide good evidence to support their argument that everyone should go to college?

College Is Not for Everyone

Michael Toomey

In the following viewpoint Michael Toomey contends that not everyone should go to college. He says college is full of kids who do not want to be there and are not interested in learning. According to Toomey, the reason they are at college is because they are "conditioned" to believe that college is for everyone. In reality, he says, college is only for the truly intellectual in society, and most people are not in this category. Toomey says that having too many nonintellectual kids attend college detracts from the college experience of people who really want to learn. Toomey is a student at the University of Massachusetts and a columnist for the university newspaper, the *Daily Collegian*.

> *"The college dream simply isn't for everyone."*

AS YOU READ, CONSIDER THE FOLLOWING QUESTIONS:

1. What percentage of students does Toomey suggest are just "trudging" through college?
2. Why do Americans crown intellectualism as a desired trait, according to Toomey?
3. What three feelings does Toomey say he has experienced at a jazz show because he was "out of his element"?

Michael Toomey, "College Dream Not for Everyone," *The Daily Collegian,* March 2, 2006. Reproduced by permission.

J ust as the high school diploma alone amounts to the difference between fry cook and greeter at Burger King, I fear that, in five years or so, an undergraduate degree will have shed more pounds than Lindsay Lohan and the Olsen twins combined.

Continuing one's education beyond that pimply, "cliquey" nightmare that is secondary school has become a fixture in the everyman's prescription for success, despite their general aversion to cerebral thought. Infesting institutions of higher learning, students with absolutely no propensity for anything academic or intellectual stare blank-faced at the walls, repeating the affirmation, "I can't wait 'til the weekend."

College Full of Disengaged, Disinterested Kids

These rather hapless young people waste millions of dollars each year, out of the pockets of parents in denial and often begrudging taxpayers, when they could and probably should be doing something vastly different. From the perspective of a relatively focused, driven young man I find the omnipresent flock of disengaged, disinterested kids to be severely irritating.

I've always experienced frustrated obligation as being palpable, which becomes burdensome when the closing words of a professor are trampled under the din of rustling backpacks and putting on of jackets, and intelligent contributions elicit a small scattering of groans. Completing high school is virtually a legal requirement and so the resentful behavior is par for the course and understandable, but technically no one binds you to attend a college or university. As academia is slowly, but surely, being jettisoned, the college experience is becoming a continuation of high school, where learning is trivially incidental to the reason you showed up.

I'd guess up to 75 percent of students trudged through high school and are continuing to drag themselves through four more years (if they make it that far). MTV's *Spring Break* and other documentations of college partying don't bode well for critics of my theory of diluted higher learning, as only in an alternate universe would bright young people join in a mass exodus to stumble foreign streets with their linguistic capabilities reduced to "Wooooo." There's probably unfortunate but overwhelming validity to the idea that college is a chance to engage in reckless, stupid behavior on your parents' dime.

Further schooling seems suited to combat this level of irresponsibility.

However, reasonable decisions are more often than not correlated to a certain level of maturity the average college student apparently has yet to reach. Note that most students become prickly when the virtue of their attendance is questioned. They will insist they have concrete goals to achieve, although their goals loiter somewhere behind checking their MySpace and obtaining illegal booze.

This perhaps suggests our educational system isn't set up appropriately; it's very linear and it seems that development is not, but what I'd identify as the monkey wrench in having schools of learners is this strange emphasis we have on being intellectual. Our operative assumption as humans is that life is something to be "figured" and the more potential you have for figuring, the higher your chances are for success.

Misguided Pursuit of Intellectualism

There's certainly plenty of evidence to support that there are certain benefits to being intellectual well-off, but there's also a whole lot of proof that falling in the average range isn't so horrible. A simple life of acceptance and assimilation works fine for most of us, but this phrase usually rings offensive because of our allegiance to being brainy.

FAST FACT

In 2007, 41 percent of college students surveyed reported engaging in binge drinking in the preceding two-week period.

Simplicity is inadequate; everyone should address the complexities of our chaotic planet, coming up with helpful and profound contributions to our understanding of it. The truth of the matter is that most people are not thinkers. Again, this reads as very politically incorrect, but it's the honest truth. There's nothing wrong with having primary concerns of good home, good food and good loving, but we like to tell ourselves otherwise.

We crown intellectualism as being a desirable trait because it's a rare one. Americans love to be unique and one-of-a-kind, and we

The National Center on Addiction and Substance Abuse at Columbia University asked students from the ages of 18 to 22 years old the following question: "Within the last month, have you engaged in binge drinking or abused prescription or other illegal drugs?"

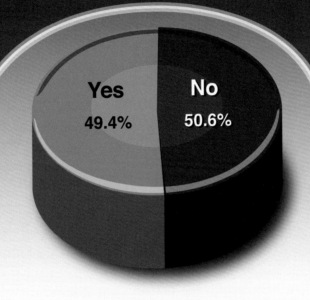

Yes
49.4%

No
50.6%

Taken from: The National Center on Addiction and Substance Abuse at Columbia University, *Wasting the Best and Brightest: Substance Abuse at America's Colleges and Universities*, March 2007.

want everyone to appreciate us for how special we are. This is by all means a relatable desire, but we go a tad overboard in trying to ensure our slice of uniqueness.

The college dream simply isn't for everyone. Very few of us are inclined towards academic learning, but the external pressure to harness coveted intellect is too strong. Many simple folk resist, resulting in a lot of placid-minded young adults creating an ironically bothersome stir in too many of our classrooms. When a person is out of his element, he can be direfully bored; he can be frustrated, he can be resentful, all because he's not on the dominant wavelength. I've experienced all these feelings at a jazz show, and although some connoisseurs of

www.CartoonStock.com

improv music may disagree, I'm not at fault for not getting jazz, nor are the musicians, nor is the audience.

It just doesn't fit in with the person I am. Maybe if everyone was giving me their two cents ("Mike, jazz is incredible, buddy; it's the real deal, man"), I might give a second listen. I might even convince myself jazz is great stuff, but I would have been conditioned into holding that opinion; it didn't originate from my own personal leanings.

"Conditioned" into College

So, in this way, conditioning has eventuated in the thinning numbers of real students in colleges and universities around the country. Excellent potential farmhands are wasting away in literature classes, talented bricklayers are toiling in statistic courses and I have a feeling this guy in my social psychology class probably makes the best Whopper the world has yet to taste.

Our fruitless stress on being the soaring eagle in all respects is keeping these kids away from their true callings, and deteriorating the quality of my classes as well. A no win situation, really. So my request, however unfeasible it may seem, is for all of us to get to know ourselves a little better, and own exactly what we find. Save your families thousands, pack up and head out towards your destiny and away from those pesky books.

EVALUATING THE AUTHOR'S ARGUMENTS:

In this viewpoint Michael Toomey argues that college is not for everyone. What evidence does he provide to support his viewpoint? Do you think some people should just be happy to be flipping burgers in a restaurant? Why or why not? Should more people accept being average?

High Schools Are Not Preparing Students for College

ACT

"There is a persistent gap between postsecondary expectations and what high schools are teaching."

In the following viewpoint the ACT contends that most U.S. high school students are unprepared for college. According to the ACT, this is not because high school students are not taking enough English, math, science, or social studies classes—the so-called core curriculum. It is because the classes they are taking are not rigorous enough. According to the ACT, teachers are not teaching and/or students are not learning what they need to know in order to succeed in college. The ACT recommends that high schools improve the quality and rigor of their core course offerings. The ACT is a nonprofit student testing and assessment organization.

Rigor at Risk. Iowa City, IA: ACT, 2007. Copyright © 2007 by ACT, Inc. All rights reserved. Reproduced by permission.

AS YOU READ, CONSIDER THE FOLLOWING QUESTIONS:
1. What did the authors of *A Nation at Risk* recommend? What year was *A Nation at Risk* published?
2. What percent of ACT-tested students does ACT say need substantial help in all four subject areas (English, mathematics, social science, and natural science) in order to be ready for college-level work?
3. According to researchers, U.S. students must possess the knowledge and skills to be able to compete with workers in other countries, especially in what two high-growth fields?

Among the motivations behind the federal government's publication of *A Nation at Risk* [in 1983] were the desire to see more students graduate from high school prepared for college and work and the need for more students to attend college. Another motivation was the importance of enabling more first-year college students to succeed in college: that is, to perform well in their courses, return to college for their second year (and beyond), and persist to a degree. The authors of *A Nation at Risk* proposed, among other recommendations, that every high school in the United States require its graduates to take a "core" curriculum: a minimum number of courses designed to provide students with a "foundation of success for the after-school year." This foundation would consist of a set of universal knowledge and skills that graduates would be able to put to good use regardless of their specific educational or work objectives.

Since then, almost every state has made significant efforts to improve its education system. Nearly a quarter-century later, in a climate in which U.S. workers are dealing with new forms of technology and facing the challenges of a global economy, it is not only reasonable but increasingly urgent to ask: Have we succeeded in fulfilling the goals of *A Nation at Risk?*

ACT research has consistently shown that high school students who take a minimum recommended core curriculum—four years of English and three years each or mathematics, science, and social studies—are likely to be more prepared for college when they graduate than are students who do not take this curriculum. Decades of research bear out this recommendation.

However, in recent years it has become increasingly apparent that, while taking the right *number* of courses is certainly better than not, it is no longer enough to guarantee that students will graduate ready for life after high school. A powerful example of this is the fact that, as defined by ACT's national college readiness indicators, the ACT College Readiness Benchmarks[1] three out of four ACT-tested 2006 high school graduates who take a core curriculum are not prepared to take credit-bearing entry-level college courses with a reasonable chance of succeeding in those courses.

These statistics for the ACT-tested high school graduating class of 2006 who took a core curriculum suggest that about one-fourth of these students are ready for college-level work in English, mathematics, social science, and natural science, while about one-fifth are not ready in any of these subject areas and the remaining students (more than half) are ready in one to three areas but not in all. Altogether, approximately 74 percent of ACT-tested 2006 high school graduates who took a core curriculum lack at least some of the skills needed for postsecondary success. Most of these students may need only a small amount of additional preparation to be ready for college, but 19 percent need substantial help in all four subject areas in order to be ready for college-level work.

FAST FACT

American high school students scored significantly lower on science literacy than students from twenty-two other countries, including Finland, Japan, Canada, China, and Germany, according to the 2006 Program for International Student Assessment.

ACT research also suggests that students today do not have a reasonable chance of becoming ready for college unless they take a number of additional higher-level courses beyond the minimum core, and that even students who do take these additional higher-level courses are not always likely to be ready for college either. This finding is in part a reflection on the quality and intensity—in other words, the *rigor*—of the high school curriculum. Without improving

1. ACT College Readiness Benchmarks are scores on the ACT test that represent the level of achievement required for students to have a high probability of college success.

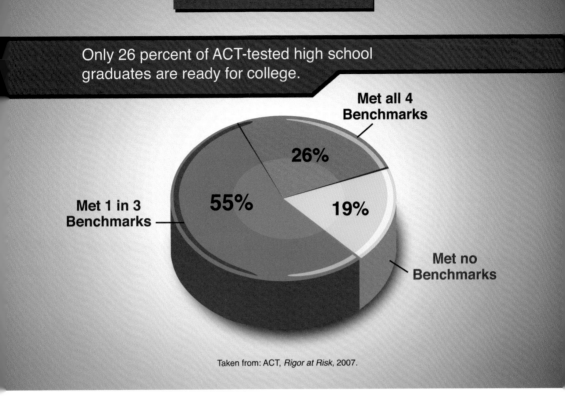

College Readiness

Only 26 percent of ACT-tested high school graduates are ready for college.

Met all 4 Benchmarks

26%

Met 1 in 3 Benchmarks

55%

19%

Met no Benchmarks

Taken from: ACT, *Rigor at Risk*, 2007.

the quality and content of the core, it appears that most students need to take additional higher-level courses to learn what they should have learned from a rigorous core curriculum, with no guarantee even then that they will be prepared for college-level work.

Is it no longer reasonable to expect, as did the authors of *A Nation at Risk*, that students should be ready for college after satisfactory completion of a core curriculum? While additional courses beyond core appear to be necessary for college readiness for many students, in the long run this is neither a reasonable expectation nor a viable strategy.

Although academic achievement is just one aspect of college readiness, it is arguably the most important one. What is now clear is that taking the right *kind* of courses matters just as much as taking the right number of courses. The academic quality and intensity of the high school curriculum is a key determinant of success in postsecondary education.

A student takes the ACT test. According to ACT Publications, teachers are not teaching and students are not learning what they need to know in order to have a successful college career.

It is neither realistic nor justifiable to expect all high school students to take more and more courses to learn what they need to learn for college. The essential agenda is to improve the quality of core courses that *really* matter in preparing students for college and work.

An unfortunate reality is that the essential foundations in our educational system needed to support a rigorous core are lacking. Most state standards do not define rigorous outcomes at the course level, so teachers are not teaching to essential course outcomes and students aren't learning them. In addition, most states do not require specific courses as prerequisites for high school graduation, thus providing insufficient direction to schools, teachers, students, or parents about what courses are important for graduation. Meanwhile, there is a persistent gap between postsecondary expectations and what high schools are teaching, and a perceptual gap in how college instructors and high school teachers view the preparedness of entering college students for college-level work. The lack of such crucial supports has a direct and dramatic impact on our students, whose chances at future success are hurt by the persistent gap between the high school experience and the more challenging requirements of postsecondary institutions.

[According to researchers,] in today's competitive global economy this gap can no longer be tolerated. U.S. students must possess the knowledge and skills to be able to compete with workers in other countries, especially in high-growth fields (such as engineering and computer technology) that require a solid mathematics and science background. . . . Without immediate improvements in educational standards, high school graduation requirements, teacher training, the alignment of elementary and secondary education with postsecondary expectations, and the vertical and horizontal alignment of high school courses, the gap between high school and postsecondary expectations may not only persist but grow larger.

So what can be done? The time has come to improve the quality of core courses so that all students have equal opportunities to become prepared for postsecondary education—whether in a two-year or four-year institution—and for work. . . .

It is time to reaffirm quality in the high school core curriculum.

EVALUATING THE AUTHOR'S ARGUMENTS:

In this viewpoint the ACT says that high school students are ill-prepared for college, and they recommend that classes be made "harder." What criteria do they use to determine that students are not prepared for college and that classes need to be more rigorous? Do you agree with their criteria? Explain. How would you rate your classes? Do you consider them to be "hard"?

No One Knows What a Good Precollege Education Is

Lynn Olson

"Pinning down what people mean by 'college readiness' and how to measure it is no easy task."

In the following viewpoint Lynn Olson contends that there is no single way to define "college readiness." The concept of college readiness is important because a large portion of students who enter college are failing to graduate. Most educators think the reason is because they entered college without the skills necessary to succeed. However, there is no consensus on how to define what those skills are. According to Olson, some educators believe placement test scores like the ACT are good indicators of college readiness, while others think grades are important. Still others believe college students need certain "habits of mind" to succeed. Olson and others suggest that coming up with an accurate definition of college readiness is important in order to increase college graduation rates. Lynn Olson is a senior education program officer at the Bill and Melinda Gates Foundation. Previously, she was a managing editor at *Education Week*.

Lynn Olson, "Views Differ on Defining College Prep," *Education Week,* April 26, 2006. Reprinted with permission from *Education Week*.

AS YOU READ, CONSIDER THE FOLLOWING QUESTIONS:
1. According to Olson, what proportion of those entering four-year colleges earn a bachelor's degree within six years?
2. What are the "habits of mind" skills that Olson says some educators think is important for college success?
3. According to Olson, what percent of first-time freshmen in four-year public institutions enroll in at least one remedial course? What is the percent for those enrolling in a two-year public institution?

One of the overarching goals of the national push to redesign high schools is increasing the number of students who graduate ready for college. Yet pinning down what people mean by "college readiness" and how to measure it is no easy task.

"It's really like the dropout issue," said Michael W. Kirst, a professor of education at Stanford University. "There are multiple definitions, with no clear consensus on which one is the most appropriate."

College Ready?

Should high school students who successfully complete a college-preparatory curriculum, for example, automatically be considered ready for higher education? What about those who score above a certain level on admissions or placement tests, or who earn good grades in high school?

Is college-readiness best defined by the skills and knowledge professors view as needed to do credit-bearing work? Or is it better thought of as the ability to avoid remedial coursework?

And what about those more elusive "habits of mind" that students bring to college, such as a willingness to cope with frustrating and ambiguous learning tasks?

Part of the problem is that the United States has more than 4,200 postsecondary institutions, ranging from two-year colleges with few admission requirements to elite research universities that take just a small fraction of their applicants. Yet few people identify what types of schools they're talking about when they use the phrase "college ready."

"I think, for the most part, people are not really defining it," said Patrick M. Callan, the president of the National Center for Public Policy and Higher Education, a nonprofit group that advocates policies to increase postsecondary opportunities and achievement, based in San Jose, Calif. To do so, he and others contend, will require a concerted, collaborative effort by those in K–12 and higher education alike.

"What we're up against now is the fruits of higher education not having participated in the whole standards movement of the 1990s," said Mr. Callan, referring to the push for state academic standards and testing for elementary and secondary students. "And so higher education, unlike K–12, in most states has very little or no tradition, and very little capacity, to act collectively on an issue like this," he said of college readiness. "I'm distressed by how far away from this we are, and how much triumphant rhetoric we hear."

College Completion Rates Driving the Discussion

Part of what's driving the discussion is a set of alarming statistics about college-completion rates. While nearly three-fourths of recent high school graduates enter some form of postsecondary education, far too many of those who start college never finish.

Of those entering four-year colleges, just over six in 10 earn a bachelor's degree within six years. The figures are worse for poor, minority, and first-generation college students and for those enrolled in two-year institutions.

Traditionally, it's been assumed that high school students who pass a core set of academic courses are ready to do college-level work. And, indeed, studies have found that taking a full slate of academically intense courses in high school—including mathematics beyond Algebra 2, and at least three years of laboratory science—increases students' chances of earning a bachelor's degree. That's led states such as Arkansas, Indiana, and Texas, as well as some school districts, to make a college-prep curriculum the default for all students.

ACT Scores Indicate Students Not Ready, but Is This Missing the Point?

But research by ACT Inc., which produces one of the nation's two major college-admissions tests, suggests that while taking a full set of

What Parents Think About College Readiness and American Schools

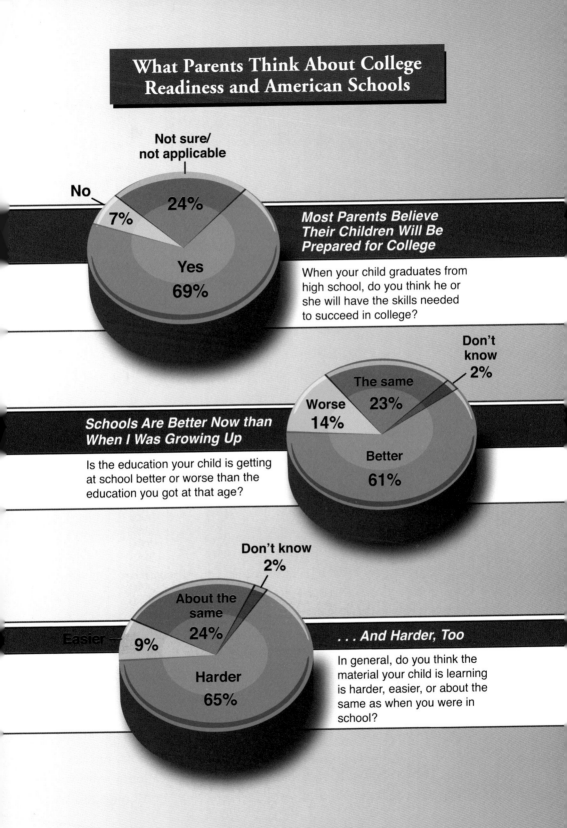

Not sure/ not applicable

No

24%

7%

Yes

69%

Most Parents Believe Their Children Will Be Prepared for College

When your child graduates from high school, do you think he or she will have the skills needed to succeed in college?

Don't know 2%

The same 23%

Worse 14%

Better 61%

Schools Are Better Now than When I Was Growing Up

Is the education your child is getting at school better or worse than the education you got at that age?

Don't know 2%

About the same 24%

Easier **9%**

Harder 65%

... And Harder, Too

In general, do you think the material your child is learning is harder, easier, or about the same as when you were in school?

Taken from: Ruth Wooden, *Reality Check 2006: Are American Parents and Students Ready for More Math and Science?* Education Insights at Public Agenda, 2006.

academic courses is important, it doesn't necessarily ensure college success.

In 2004, the Iowa City, Iowa–based nonprofit organization looked at the relationships between high school coursetaking, ACT scores, and students' grades in college. The ACT defined college readiness as having a 75 percent chance of earning a C or better, and a 50 percent chance of earning a B or better, in four common first-year courses.

FAST FACT

As of the 2005–2006 school year, 14.2 million computers, or one for every four students, were available for classroom use in the nation's schools, according to the U.S. Census Bureau.

It found, for example, that students who scored a 22 out of a possible 36 on the ACT math test were likely to earn at least a C in college algebra. But only 13 percent of students who had completed high school math through Algebra 2, and only 37 percent who had completed math through trigonometry, achieved the score that the ACT identified as ready for college-level work.

"It does call to question whether our courses are at an appropriate level of rigor," said Cyndie Schmeiser, the ACT's senior vice president for research and development. "When students take Algebra 1, Algebra 2, and geometry courses in high school, why aren't they ready for a college algebra course?"

Yet defining college readiness in terms of a cutoff score on a college-admissions test may be missing the point, says David S. Spence, the president of the Southern Regional Education Board, based in Atlanta. "It's as if, as long as we test all these students and tell them whether they're ready according to a score, that that's going to get them ready," he said. "The thing is to back up and make sure these standards are fully part of the curriculum."

What About Grades?

A study tracking graduates of the Chicago public schools, released last week [April 2006], found that grades in core academic courses were a more important predictor of college enrollment and graduation than scores on admissions exams. "Grades are an indicator of students' ability to complete assignments and prepare high-quality work, something necessary for success in college," explained co-author Elaine M. Allensworth, an associate director at the Consortium on Chicago School Research at the University of Chicago.

Habits of Mind

Other efforts to define college readiness have brought together higher education faculty members to identify what entering students need to know.

Among them was a two-year study by Standards for Success, a project of the Association of American Universities and the Philadelphia-based Pew Charitable Trusts, at the University of Oregon. It brought together more than 400 faculty and staff members from 20 leading research universities to identify what students must do to succeed in entry-level, credit-bearing courses at those institutions. The resulting standards were published in 2003 with a document that offered samples of college work up to the standards.

Standards for Success developed two sets of standards, one for all students and one for potential majors in particular subjects. While the standards focus on English, math, science, social science, second languages, and the arts, one of the dominant themes is the importance of the "habits of mind" students need to acquire in high school and bring with them to college.

Those include critical thinking, analytical thinking, and problem-solving; an inquisitive nature; the willingness to accept critical feedback and to adjust on the basis of that feedback; openness to possible failures from time to time; and the ability and desire to cope with frustrating and ambiguous learning tasks.

Other critical skills include the ability to express oneself in writing and orally, to discern the relative importance and credibility of various sources of information, to draw inferences and reach conclusions independently, and to use technology as a tool for learning.

"Our finding, which has been replicated in a half-dozen other studies we've done, is that higher education faculty emphasize ways of thinking as much as or more than specific content knowledge," said David T. Conley, the University of Oregon professor of educational leadership and policy who led the study. "In my opinion, that might be the largest single disconnect between high school and college."

Surveys of college professors and K–12 educators have found large gaps between how well prepared high school teachers think their students are for college and what college faculty members think. A survey released last month by *The Chronicle of Higher Education*, for example, found that while 31 percent of high school teachers believed their students were "very well" prepared for college-level work, only 13 percent of professors agreed.

The problem with such surveys, said Mr. Kirst of Stanford, "is I've been following what college professors say about students for 30 years, and they're never happy. I don't know what it takes to satisfy those people. To me, it tends to be what the ideal student would look like, rather than someone who could pass the work."

He added that most efforts to identify entry-level prerequisites have not focused on community colleges, which enroll 45 percent of undergraduates. Just identifying the common entry-level courses at such institutions is hard, he said.

In an institution with five levels of college English and three levels of remedial reading, Mr. Kirst said, "Which one is college-ready?"

Remediation Free?

One reason for the concern about college readiness is the large proportion of high school graduates who end up taking remedial courses in college for which they earn no credit—at considerable cost to themselves and to their institutions. Research has found that those who take two or more remedial courses are unlikely to graduate.

"I think colleges are more and more recognizing that they have a role to play in this," said Gaston Caperton, the president of the New York–based College Board, home of both the SAT college-admissions exam and the Advanced Placement program. "One of the things that colleges recognize is that they don't want to bring all their kids in and have to serve as a remedial program. That's not what they're there for."

But experts caution against defining college readiness as the ability to avoid any remedial courses—starting with the fact that it's so hard to identify what's a remedial course and what's not, and to get a firm fix on remediation rates. Moreover, a student may need remediation

The organization Standards for Success at the University of Oregon has developed two sets of standards, one for all students and one for potential majors.

in writing but not in reading, or in math but not in biology. At what point is the student "college ready"?

Depending on the source, estimates are that between 28 percent and 40 percent of first-time freshmen in four-year public institutions, and between 42 percent and 63 percent of first-time freshmen in two-year public institutions, enroll in at least one remedial course.

In most states, individual colleges and universities select their own placement tests and their own standards for how well students must perform to avoid remediation, sending mixed messages to incoming students. . . .

Beyond Academics

Some studies and programs have begun to follow high school graduates into college to look at the factors that contribute to students' success. And they've identified a set of skills that go beyond traditional academics.

AVID, for Advancement Via Individual Determination, is a secondary school program that prepares underachieving students, primarily those who are African-American and Latino, for success in four-year colleges. The program is now in nearly 2,300 schools nationwide and around the world. Three-quarters of 2004 AVID graduates were accepted to four-year colleges and, according to the program's founder, Mary Catherine Swanson, nearly nine in 10 AVID graduates re-enroll for sophomore year fully academically qualified.

"So what is it that they have learned?" Ms. Swanson said. "We have been able to give them the study skills and the resiliency skills to be able to succeed."

Part of that preparation, she argues, is making students savvy consumers of higher education. "Our students tell us, so many of the colleges now have professors whose first language isn't English, and it's hard for the kids to understand," she said as an example. "Also, a lot of the professors' teaching skills, quite frankly, are not what they are in high schools.

"We make the kids learn how to be advocates for themselves because we teach them no system is going to be totally fair." AVID graduates, for example, know how to work collaboratively and to reach out for help, rather than thinking they can handle college on their own. The program also works with students and their families, beginning in grade 6, on how to pay for college. And it provides practical guidance on the college-search and -application process.

Research by Mr. Kirst and others has found that minority and first-generation college students, in particular, may lack information about what's needed for college preparation and admissions.

Ms. Swanson's perspective echoes findings from two New York studies—one following the graduates from a group of 28 small public high schools, and the other following graduates from one small high school.

"I do think the way we're talking about college readiness has been way too narrowly defined," argued Lori Chajet, a doctoral student at the City University of New York Graduate Center who is conducting one of the studies. "More often than not, when people think about college readiness, they think almost exclusively about academic preparation."

While that's necessary, she said, it's not sufficient. "In my reading, most of this K–16 pipeline people are talking about is about matching up standardized tests, and that's missing so much of the larger picture," Ms. Chajet said.

And students' success in college depends on the postsecondary institutions they attend as well as the high schools they graduate from. One study, by the Washington-based Education Trust, a research and advocacy group that focuses on the education of disadvantaged students, found that even colleges that are similar have graduation rates that vary by as much as 30 percentage points or more.

Among other factors, the study by Kevin Carey found, colleges with better completion rates focused on getting students engaged and connected to campus starting freshman year, emphasized the quality of undergraduate teaching and learning, monitored student progress, and made student success a top institutional priority.

EVALUATING THE AUTHORS' ARGUMENTS:

In this viewpoint Lynn Olson contends that college readiness cannot be defined in one single way. In the previous viewpoint ACT says most students are not prepared for college. What does Olson say about defining college readiness based on ACT scores? Do ACT and Olson agree on anything? After reading the two viewpoints, how would you define college readiness?

Advanced Placement Classes Are Beneficial

Jay Mathews

"A team of Texas researchers have concluded the difficult courses and three-hour exams [for Advanced Placement courses] are worth it."

In the following viewpoint Jay Mathews looks in depth at two research studies that showed that Advanced Placement (AP) courses help students in college. Mathews asks experts to comment on what the studies say about how AP students match up with non-AP students, whether AP classes deserve college credit, and the importance of taking AP exams, not just AP courses. Mathews believes taking AP courses and exams helps students become better learners and harder workers, and this benefits them in college. Jay Mathews is the education reporter for the *Washington Post*.

AS YOU READ, CONSIDER THE FOLLOWING QUESTIONS:

1. According to Mathews, what were the sizes of the two Texas studies?
2. How did the Texas studies attempt to address the problem of selection bias, as stated by Mathews?
3. According to the author, why should students be encouraged to take AP courses *and* exams?

Jay Mathews, "New Studies Say AP Works," *Washington Post,* January 30, 2007. Copyright © 2007 *The Washington Post.* Reprinted with permission.

The College Board releases its annual *Advanced Placement Report to the Nation* next week. For us AP and IB dorks, it is the equivalent of the State of the Union address. No, delete that. The State of the Union is usually a bore. AP's *Report to the Nation* is more like the Academy Awards, for a small group of socially awkward fans like me.

For those of you new to this obsession, Advanced Placement and International Baccalaureate are courses and tests given to high school students that are designed to be the equivalent of introductory college courses in about two dozen subjects. They impress selective-college admissions offices. If the students do well on the tests, they can earn college credits and skip introductory courses for more advanced stuff when they get to college.

Texas Researchers Report AP Worth It

This year there was a bonus in the *Report to the Nation*. In the advance copy for reporters, I saw a reference to two new studies of AP in Texas that appeared to break new ground. Since these were reports by independent researchers, I was not breaking the College Board embargo if I sought them out and asked to see their work.

The result was a story I wrote for yesterday's [January 29, 2007] editions of *The Post*. Here are the first paragraphs:

> In the midst of a national debate over whether Advanced Placement courses place too much pressure on American high school students, a team of Texas researchers have concluded the difficult courses and three-hour exams are worth it.

> In the largest study ever of the impact of AP on college success, which looked at 222,289 students from all backgrounds attending a wide range of Texas universities, the researchers said they found "strong evidence of benefits to students who participate in both AP courses and exams in terms of higher GPAs, credit hours earned, and four-year graduation rates."

> A separate University of Texas study of 24,941 students said those who used their AP credits to take more advanced courses in college had better grades in those courses than similar students who took college introductory courses instead of AP in ten different subjects.

"Both of these papers are home runs. They definitely settle a lot," said Joseph Hawkins, an AP expert who is senior study director for the private research firm Westat in Rockville.

The new studies run counter to an unpublished Harvard and University of Virginia study that casts doubt on the worth of AP science courses, and contradict some critics who say that high school courses, even with an AP label, cannot match the depth of the college introductory courses. . . .

In-Depth Look at the Studies

I want to use the extra space here, cruelly denied me whenever I write a news story for the paper, to identify what I think are the most interesting parts, and to let the experts I consulted have more than the paltry 56 words—I just counted—that I had room to quote in the news story.

Students in California attend an Advanced Placement biology class. Researchers say that AP courses and exams benefit students with higher grade averages and increased four-year graduation rates.

Comparing AP Students with Non-AP Students

Both studies attempted to put this competition on a level playing field by comparing the college success of AP students to those non-AP students (or AP students who did not take the AP exam) who were similar in important ways. The larger study, by University of Texas—Austin researchers Linda Hargrove and Barbara Dodd and Texas Higher Education Coordinating Board researcher Donn Godin, compared students with about the same SAT or ACT scores, or similar family economic circumstances.

Selection Bias

But Saul Geiser, the University of California scholar who produced his own massive AP and college success study in 2004, said these comparisons are still a problem.

The main technical issue that bedevils not only the Texas studies but all research of this kind concerns the question of selection bias: To what extent is AP students' success in college a reflection of the AP program itself (a "program effect") as opposed to the personal characteristics of the students selected for the program (a "selection effect")? . . . This question is particularly important in evaluating AP because the program historically has targeted "better," academically stronger students who could be expected to perform well in college even without AP.

Both of the Texas studies attempt to address the problem of selection bias by "matching" AP and non-AP students on other measures, primarily SAT scores, in order to control for student background characteristics. But neither study controls for a sufficiently robust set of student characteristics to rule out the hypothesis that selection effects account for most of the relationship between AP and college outcomes. The larger study of all Texas public institutions by Hargrove, Godin and Dodd matched AP and non-AP students only on two measures, SAT I scores and participation in free-lunch programs, while the smaller study matched students only on SAT I scores and high-school class rank. As a result, the studies control for far fewer variables than previous researchers have considered, leaving open the possibility, and indeed probability, that systematic differences in student motivation, academic preparation, family background and high-school quality account for much of the observed difference in college outcomes between AP and non-AP students.

AP Deserving of College Credit

This is the part of the second Texas study, by University of Texas—Austin researchers Leslie Keng and Barbara Dodd, that attempts to shed light in the so far clueless debate over whether AP and IB students deserve college credit and a chance to skip to a more advanced college course.

Many selective schools allow only students with the highest grade, a 5, on the AP exam to get credit. Some insist that their introductory courses are so special that no AP grade is high enough. But the amount of research they have devoted to proving their point is laughingly small. Harvard made a rule that only 5s will count—and only if a student is going for sophomore standing—based on one study of three courses that showed AP students not doing as well as students who first took the college's intro course. A few colleges have data from a similarly small number of courses that show the AP or IB students do better on the advanced course than students who have taken the college's intro course. But most colleges have no data. When you ask them on what they rest their restrictive rules, they shrug and say the faculty wanted it that way.

The Texas study has to be read very carefully, because although it concludes that students who received AP credit in 10 subjects at UT did better in the advanced course than students who first took the intro course, picking the right advanced course for the researchers to gather data from and study was difficult, and in some cases, with some categories of student, the triumph of the AP kids is not so clear. . . .

FAST FACT

The greatest percentage of graduating seniors scoring 3+ on an AP exam in high school, according to the College Board, were in New York (23.4 percent), Virginia (21.5 percent), and Florida (20.3 percent).

AP Exams Are Important

Geiser shares with me, and most of the AP teachers I know, the view that AP students should be encouraged to take the AP exams. This

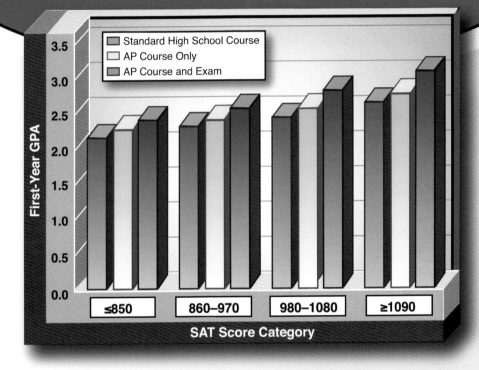

The First-Year College GPA of AP Students Is Higher than Non-AP Students

Legend:
- Standard High School Course
- AP Course Only
- AP Course and Exam

First-Year GPA

SAT Score Category: ≤850, 860–970, 980–1080, ≥1090

Taken from: College Board, *Advanced Placement Report to the Nation*, 2007.
Based on data from Leslie Keng and Barbara Dodd, "An Investigation of College Performance of AP and Non-AP Student Groups," University of Texas at Austin, 2007.

is sometimes difficult because the seniors who often take AP have their exams scheduled in May, after they have gotten into college, after the weather has turned warm, and just as the season of prom/senior-cut-day/senior-prank-day/senioritis extremis reaches its peak.

The Texas researchers, like Geiser and others who have looked at this, have convincing evidence that it is working hard to understand the material and getting good grades on the AP exams that correlates with college success, not just taking the course. . . .

AP vs. Dual Enrollment

Dual enrollment—a common term for courses taken at local colleges, or conducted by local colleges, for high school students—takes a major hit in the Keng-Dodd study. The researchers say students who took dual enrollment courses in high school did not do as well in college as those who took AP courses.

This is a very important issue, worthy of another column as soon as dual enrollment's defenders get a chance to read the full report. I have been talking about the relative rigor of AP, IB and dual enrollment with many educators who think *Newsweek's* America's Best High Schools list should count dual enrollment courses, as it now counts AP and IB exams. The Keng-Dodd data convinces me *Newsweek* needs a lot more information before it takes that step.

Former U.S. Education Department researcher Cliff Adelman, the guru of college completion data, had these thoughts:

> I am not overly surprised that dual-enrollment courses don't have the same impact as AP. I'll put good money on the table that dual-enrollment courses are capturing a somewhat different population. What would be interesting would be to compare the education histories of students who took dual-enrollment course X at a local community college while in high school with those who entered the community college and took it there, and then to divide the latter group into those who transferred to the 4-year sector and those who didn't. . . .

AP Makes Students Better Learners

What does it all mean? It will take some time to figure that out. There is too much data here to absorb all at once, and we are likely to see an acceleration of research on AP and IB, given their growing importance, that is going to make it hard for even us devotees to keep up.

One of my favorite fellow AP addicts is Hawkins, the senior study director I quoted in my news article yesterday. He is an educational activist who has made a study of AP results among minority students. His view on these numbers has strongly influenced my thinking. He believes that it is not so much what is learned in AP, but the act of struggling with a difficult course that adds the most value.

"So taking AP courses and exams is highly associated with college outcomes down the road," he said, summing up this research.

"But I think this happens not just because the kids who take these courses learn stuff and master knowledge (college level stuff), but because these kids also in the process become better learners, students, scholars. They end up mastering the importance of working hard, clearly something that will serve them well in college and later in life."

That seems right to me, but I await the next deluge of data to see if Hawkins can be proved right.

EVALUATING THE AUTHOR'S ARGUMENTS:

In this viewpoint Jay Mathews says that studies show that Advanced Placement (AP) programs are worth the effort. Can you identify parts of Mathew's viewpoint that are objective? Can you identify parts of his viewpoint that are subjective? Is Mathew's opinion within the viewpoint obvious or subtle? Explain.

Advanced Placement Classes Are Not Beneficial

Tom Stanley-Becker

"As an AP dropout, I hope to go to college on a road more meandering and slowly traveled."

In the following viewpoint Tom Stanley-Becker contends that the Advanced Placement (AP) program is too much about taking tests and not enough about learning. He says he dropped out of his AP history course and is glad he did. Now, instead of focusing his learning on what "might be included" on an AP exam, he can really learn about history. Another reason not to take AP courses, says Stanley-Becker, is because colleges do not grant credit for them anyway. Tom Stanley-Becker is a student at the University of Chicago's University High School and an editor for his school newspaper.

AS YOU READ, CONSIDER THE FOLLOWING QUESTIONS:
1. According to Stanley-Becker, what organization administers the AP program?
2. What does the author say was the originating idea behind the AP program? When did the program originate?
3. Stanley-Becker compares the education of those in the AP program with the production of what?

Tom Stanley-Becker, "Bursting the AP Bubble," *Los Angeles Times,* May 8, 2008. Reproduced by permission of the author.

I'm an AP dropout. When classmates in my Advanced Placement U.S. history course take the AP exam Friday, I won't be with them. When they pick up their pencils and start filling in those little bubbles, I'll be reading the words of George Kennan, Lillian Hellman, Harry Truman and Paul Robeson—for a paper I'm writing on the Cold War.

No Time to *Learn*

The problem with the AP program is that we don't have time to really learn U.S. history because we're preparing for the exam. We race through the textbook, cramming in the facts, a day on the Great Awakening, a week on the Civil War and Reconstruction, a week on World War II, a week on the era from FDR to JFK, a day on the civil rights movement—with nothing on transcendentalism, or the Harlem Renaissance, or Albert Einstein. There is no time to write a paper. Bound by the exam, my history teacher wistfully says we have to be ready in early May.

The author contends that the Advanced Placement program, like this advanced art program in California, is more about passing the AP test than preparing students for college.

Sometimes I feel as if the College Board, which administers the AP program, is haunting our history class—a long, gray, flat board with a clock on it looming over us. Like an oracle, it tells us what is worth learning and how long learning should take.

The overriding goal is to crack the AP test. That means taking a lot of practice tests—week after week, filling in those bubbles in class. It means researching past AP exams to predict what will be on the test. It means answering model AP essay questions for homework. It means brute memorization. My classmates ask: Will there be more questions on the American Revolution or World War I? What do we really have to know about mercantilism? Their unspoken question is: If I blow the AP test, can I still get into a good college?

In class, we cannot stray from the AP regimen. A few weeks ago, we were rushing through the 1960s with lightning speed. The Vietnam War is a fog. Somehow the New Frontier turned into the Great Society, which I always confuse with the New Freedom, the New Nationalism and the New Federalism. And what does CORE stand for?

FAST FACT

AP U.S. history was the most frequently taken AP exam by the 2007 high school graduating class, according to the College Board.

But what really caught my eye was something in the textbook about a 1970 women's liberation march down Fifth Avenue in New York, where some marchers burned their bras. Why was it radical to burn a bra, I wondered? But there was no time for this in class.

When the AP program originated in the early 1950s, the idea was to offer a rich curriculum of advanced work, bridging the senior year of high school with college. It was the brainchild of educators at colleges and prep schools, based on two studies funded by the Ford Foundation. The Educational Testing Service administered the first AP exams in 1954, with the College Board taking over in 1955. Today, the program promises a ticket to college admission and college credits through its 37 "college-level" AP courses and exams (in 22 subject areas), as diverse as physics and studio art, most taken by juniors.

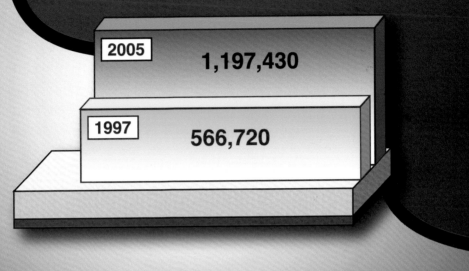

Number of American High School Students Taking AP Examinations

2005   1,197,430

1997   566,720

Taken from: The College Board Advanced Placement Program, *National Summary Reports*, 1997–2005.

Assembly Line Education

But in applying to college, my classmates are learning that many schools grant no AP credits at all—even for a perfect exam score of 5—and others only for some subjects. So, with nearly 1.4 million students worldwide taking 2.5 million AP exams in 2007—300,000 in U.S. history—the reality is becoming clear: AP classes have simply become another credential for college admission.

Instead of studying history, we study for the AP exam: And along the way, our education has come to resemble the production of Model Ts on Ford's assembly line, with the College Board cracking down by auditing AP syllabuses before allowing schools to put the official AP trademark on student transcripts.

So I became an AP dropout; and I'm not alone. According to *Education Week*, since 2006, more than 2,000 high schools across the country and around the world have dropped the AP curriculum to march to their own drummers.

Meanwhile, freed from the AP regime as the exam approached, I slowed down to do independent research.

Sometimes I wonder how I would do on the AP exam—but not for long. As an AP dropout, I hope to go to college on a road more meandering and slowly traveled.

EVALUATING THE AUTHORS' ARGUMENTS:

In this viewpoint Tom Stanley-Becker contends that the Advanced Placement (AP) program is not beneficial for students going to college. In the previous viewpoint Jay Mathews says the AP program is beneficial. Which viewpoint do you think was better supported? Which argument do you think was more persuasive and why? Was it the one that you thought was better supported?

Chapter 2

How Should High School Students Decide Where to Go to College?

As part of her college selection process, a student reviews copies of acceptance letters from four universities.

Viewpoint 1

The *U.S. News & World Report* College Rankings Are Helpful

Robert Morse

"When U.S. News started the college and university rankings 25 years ago [1983], no one imagined that these lists would become what some consider to be the 800-pound gorilla of American higher education."

In the following viewpoint Robert Morse says the *U.S. News & World Report* college rankings are an important tool for helping students decide which college to attend. Morse says when the rankings were devised, back in 1983, *U.S. News* editors knew they were needed, but they had no idea how important they would become. Morse says the reason the rankings are so important is because they help students make one of the most important and costly decisions of their lives—that is deciding which one of the over thirteen hundred, four-year American colleges to attend. Robert Morse has been at the helm of the *U.S. News & World Report* education rankings since 1987.

Robert Morse, "The Birth of the College Rankings," *U.S. News & World Report,* May 16, 2008. Copyright © 2008 U.S. News & World Report, L.P. All rights reserved. Reprinted with permission.

AS YOU READ, CONSIDER THE FOLLOWING QUESTIONS:
1. According to Morse, what "national university" was ranked number one in the first *U.S. News* college rankings?
2. What has been the biggest shift in the rankings formula, as stated by Morse?
3. According to the author, when did the *U.S. News* graduate-school rankings debut?

When *U.S. News* started the college and university rankings 25 years ago [1983], no one imagined that these lists would become what some consider to be the 800-pound gorilla of American higher education, important enough to be the subject of doctoral dissertations, academic papers and conferences, endless debate, and constant media coverage. What began with little fanfare has spawned imitation college rankings in at least 21 countries, including Canada, China, Britain, Germany, Poland, Russia, Spain, and Taiwan.

Filling a Void

Today, it's hard to imagine there ever was a void of information to help people make direct comparisons between colleges, but such was the case in 1983 when we first ventured into the field. The editors back then, led by Marvin L. Stone, thought the project was worth attempting because a college education is one of the most important—and most costly— investments that people ever make. (Of course, that perspective is even more relevant today when the price of an undergraduate education at some private universities hovers in the $200,000 range.) So the magazine designed a survey and sent it out to 1,308 college presidents to get their opinions of which schools offered the best education. The winners: Stanford (National Universities) and Amherst (National Liberal Arts Colleges).

> **FAST FACT**
>
> Within seventy-two hours of the release of the 2007 *U.S. News & World Report* College Rankings, the *U.S. News* Web site received 10 million page views, according to one of the magazine's editors.

According to a U.S. News & World Report *survey, Stanford University in Palo Alto, California, is the nation's top university in academics.*

That academic-reputation-only method was repeated in 1985 and 1987. In 1988, we started to use statistical data as part of the ranking methodology, evaluating those numbers along with the results of the survey. In 1997, in another pioneering step, the America's Best Colleges rankings made the leap online at usnews.com. The online version, viewed by millions, has substantially more information and extended rankings than there is room for in the magazine.

Change with Times

Of course, we've changed the ranking formula over the years to reflect changes in the world of higher education. In general, the biggest shift has been the move toward evaluating colleges less by the quality of the students they attract (inputs) and more by the success the school has in graduating those students (outputs). We operate under the guiding principle that the methodology should be altered only if the change will better help our readers compare schools as they're making decisions about where to apply and enroll.

It helps to have this principle to focus on when the inevitable criticisms of the rankings and their influence arise. Chief among the criticisms is the idea that it is impossible to reduce the experience that any given college has to offer to a number on a list. A fair enough observation, but one that does little to help the student who will have to choose just one to attend. Another criticism of the rankings is that they often substitute as a sort of performance evaluation measure for the school and its employees. *U.S. News* is keenly aware that the higher education community is also a major audience and consumer of our rankings. We understand how seriously academics, administrators, and governing boards study and analyze our rankings and how they use them in various ways, including benchmarking alumni fundraising, and advertising to attract students.

Expansion

Based on the success of the college rankings, we decided to expand the process to other levels of education. The America's Best Graduate

Factors Considered in the *U.S. News* Rankings and the "Weight" Given to Each Factor

- 10%
- 5%
- 5%
- 25%
- 20%
- 20%
- 15%

- Peer Assessment
- Retention
- Faculty Resources
- Student Selectivity
- Financial Resources
- Graduation Rate Performance
- Alumni Giving

Taken from: *U.S. News & World Report*, 2007.

Schools rankings debuted in 1990 with annual listings of medical, engineering, law, business, and education schools.

Our newest education ranking is America's Best High Schools, first published in the fall of 2007. It identified the 100 best public schools out of more than 18,000 across the nation. Just as when we embarked on college rankings, setting up the process wasn't easy, but it's already proved to have enormous weight with our readers.

EVALUATING THE AUTHOR'S ARGUMENTS:

In this viewpoint Robert Morse says the *U.S. News* college rankings are helpful, and he explains how they were originally designed. How were rankings determined? Do think this is a good methodology? If you were to design a college ranking methodology, what would be the number one factor you would consider?

The *U.S. News & World Report* College Rankings Are Flawed

Peyton R. Helm

"The U.S. News *rankings may organize some useful information in an easy-to-read format; but as a tool for choosing the right college they are seriously flawed."*

In the following viewpoint Peyton R. Helm contends that the *U.S. News & World Report* college rankings are based on a flawed methodology. Helm thinks the *U.S. News* rankings are too heavily based on reputation and the amount of money schools have to spend. He believes rich schools can buy a top-five ranking. Helm contends that it is impossible to determine the single best college for everyone because there are so many factors to consider when choosing a college, and different people value different things. Helm thinks the most helpful "college decision" tool would be one that lets each prospective student consider different schools according to the factors they think are most important. Peyton R. Helm is a history professor and the president of Muhlenberg College, a private liberal arts college located in Allentown, Pennsylvania.

Peyton R. Helm, "'Hearsay' Isn't the Way to Choose a College," *The Morning Call,* June 29, 2007. Copyright © 2007 The Morning Call, Inc. Reproduced by permission.

AS YOU READ, CONSIDER THE FOLLOWING QUESTIONS:
1. List the factors that Helm says students use to weigh the choice of a college, but which are not considered in the *U.S. News* rankings.
2. According to Helm, what factor considered in *U.S. News* rankings is based on institutional wealth but has a direct bearing on educational quality?
3. The Web-based tool that Helm says he and other college leaders are working on will lay out essential statistics on what factors?

America loves competition and America loves lists. They do little or no harm and are often lots of fun. Think World Series, *American Idol*, and David Letterman. So what's wrong with the *U.S. News & World Report* college rankings? And why will I be working with other college presidents and educational organizations to develop an alternative rather than filling out the magazine's absurd survey next year?

The answer is really not that complicated. *U.S. News* claims that the annual college rankings issue (which many claim is their biggest seller and moneymaker) provides an important tool to parents and students engaged in searching for the "best" college or university. Nonsense. That's like saying *People Magazine*'s "10 Most Eligible Bachelors" list provides an important tool to women looking for a husband.

No Single "Best"

The fact is, high school seniors are so tremendously varied in their interests, talents, personalities, and abilities that there is no single way of measuring what is "best" for all of them. Distance from home, range of majors and other programs of study, athletic and extracurricular options, learning outcomes, campus atmosphere, and graduate and professional school placement rates—all are important factors for students weighing the choice of a college, and none are considered in the *U.S. News* rankings.

Instead, 25 percent of the magazine's ratings—the most heavily weighted single factor—is based on the so-called "reputational survey" in which college presidents, deans, and deans of admission rate other institutions on a five-point scale from inadequate to very good. But what are we really evaluating?

I know my own college, Muhlenberg, very well of course. I know it's unmatched for a close and supportive campus atmosphere, great liberal arts teaching, and our graduates' impressive success rate in obtaining jobs and admission to medical, law, and other graduate and professional schools. But even a great college like Muhlenberg isn't

Critics of the U.S. News & World Report *college survey say its rankings are flawed because wealthy schools, such as Harvard, have massive endowments.*

right for everybody. The student who wants to major in engineering or play Division I football or live in a large urban campus would not find what she or he is looking for with us.

Most of the 260 or so schools in my survey are totally unfamiliar to me, so I check "N/A." But what of the handful of institutions I do know fairly well? What am I supposed to be evaluating? Their curricula? Their facilities? The quality of the food in their dining halls? Apparently I am supposed to rate their "reputations"—and what is my knowledge based on? Rumors, hearsay, time-worn memories from when I was applying to college a generation ago, or vague impressions gathered when my sons were on the college search trail a few years ago?

Richer Schools Ranked Higher

Most of the other factors weighted by *U.S. News* in their rankings (in a secret formula they will not reveal, that is changed every year, and that independent researchers have been unable to replicate) are based, ultimately, on institutional wealth. A few of these (such as faculty-student ratio) have a direct bearing on educational quality. A few (such as SAT score ranges for admitted students) may provide helpful guidance as to whether a student has a good chance of admission.

FAST FACT

Princeton University was ranked first among national universities by *U.S. News & World Report* for eight years in a row, from 2001 to 2008.

The *U.S. News* rankings may organize some useful information in an easy-to-read format; but as a tool for choosing the right college they are seriously flawed. Most of the data simply reflects the size of institutions' endowments [gifts of money] and fundraising muscle—not how effectively those resources are deployed. A trustee once asked me what it would take for Muhlenberg to be ranked in the top five by *U.S. News.* My answer was simple: A check for $800 million placed directly in the endowment would do it—even if we never changed another thing we were doing.

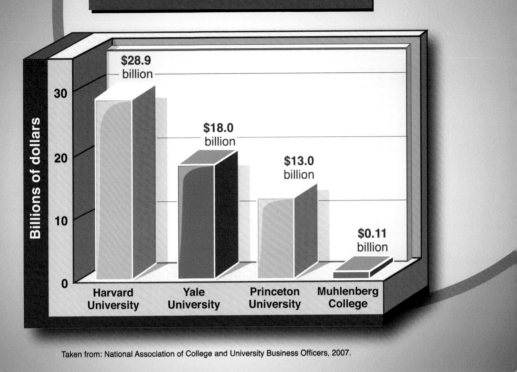

College Endowments, 2006

Billions of dollars

$28.9 billion — Harvard University

$18.0 billion — Yale University

$13.0 billion — Princeton University

$0.11 billion — Muhlenberg College

Taken from: National Association of College and University Business Officers, 2007.

What you won't read in *U.S. News* is that most of the data they use is public information, readily available on the Web sites of most colleges and universities, as well as on the U.S. Department of Education Web site. There is no single formula for weighting these factors—they will have different significance for different students and families.

Working on a Better Tool

So, next year I and many other leaders of our nation's best colleges and universities will be working on a new and better Web-based tool for families engaged in the college search, laying out essential statistics on admissions, costs, financial aid, majors and degree programs, diversity, campus life, graduation rates, and post-graduate options. Families can weigh each of these factors according to their own needs, interests, and priorities. Our tool will not have the razzle-dazzle of the Super Bowl or the Miss America contest, but it will provide a standardized, transparent, and easily accessible snapshot of key information that families need to make this important decision. I expect this will keep me busy, so don't expect to see me on *Dancing with the Stars.*

EVALUATING THE AUTHORS' ARGUMENTS:

What is the main reason Peyton R. Helm argues that the *U.S. News & World Report* college rankings are flawed? What evidence does he use to support his contention? After reading Helm's viewpoint and the previous viewpoint by Robert Morse, do you think the *U.S. News & World Report* rankings are helpful or not? Use examples from the viewpoints to support your answer.

Students Should Look for Colleges That Prepare Them for the Real World

Richard M. Freeland

"Families and students should remember that college is both an experience in itself and a building block of a total life structure."

In the following viewpoint Richard M. Freeland advises students to choose colleges that provide opportunities for real-world experiences along with their academic offerings. Freeland believes that for many students the college experience is disconnected from the path of life. After four years of college these students still do not know who they are, where they are going, or even what they want to be. Freeland believes that students should view college as just one step in the path of life. Students should choose colleges that offer structured, well-supported internships or other real-world experiences that help prepare them for life after they graduate. Richard M. Freeland is a distinguished professor of higher education at Clark University and president emeritus of Northeastern University.

Richard M. Freeland, "A Better Way to Choose a College," *Christian Science Monitor,* January 10, 2008. Copyright © 2008 *The Christian Science Monitor.* All rights reserved. Reproduced by permission of the author.

AS YOU READ, CONSIDER THE FOLLOWING QUESTIONS:
1. According to Freeland, what is a "boomerang" student?
2. What does Freeland say is one of the great shortcomings of many of the nation's leading colleges and universities?
3. According to the author, what do Stanford University, Tulane, and Notre Dame do to help students prepare for real life? How about Northeastern University, Cincinnati, and Georgia Tech?

This is a time of year [January] when high school students and their families are thinking hard about college. As seniors, juniors, and parents identify their top choices, discussions typically focus on the college itself. Is the institution small or large? How strong are the academics? What is the social life like? Do I like the campus?

Such considerations are important, but they can obscure the all-important question: Where will these college years lead?

Applicants should think seriously about which college on their list can best prepare them for the real world. They should look for campuses that offer well-structured programs to help them form a direction for their lives and develop the capacity to take steps along that path.

FAST FACT

In 2006 about 46 percent of full-time college students ages 16–24 were employed, according to the U.S. Census Bureau.

The Boomerang Student

One of the most striking regent phenomena about college graduates in America has been the "boomerang" student: the young person who goes away to college, has a great experience, graduates, then moves back home for a year or two to figure out what to do with his or her life. This pattern has left many graduates—and their families—wondering whether it makes sense to spend four or more years at college, often at great expense, and finish with no clear sense of who they are or what they want to do next.

The trend points to one of the great shortcomings of many of our nation's leading colleges and universities. Structured, mentored opportunities to think about life after graduation are rare. The formal curriculum focuses almost universally on the academic disciplines of the arts and sciences. Advising on how various majors connect to pathways into the workplace is typically haphazard. Career planning offices are often understaffed and marginal to college life.

It doesn't need to be this way, and in recent years some of the country's top colleges have enriched their academic offerings with opportunities for students to gain real-world experiences.

Colleges Can Help Students Obtain Real-World Experiences

Stanford University, Tulane, and Notre Dame have developed outstanding programs through which students work in community settings to develop skills in active citizenship. Leading co-op schools such as Northeastern University, Cincinnati, and Georgia Tech place students in multiple full-time work experiences related to their majors during their college careers. Clark University empowers students to "make a difference by linking classroom study with

Notre Dame is one of several universities that has programs through which students work in community settings to develop citizenship skills.

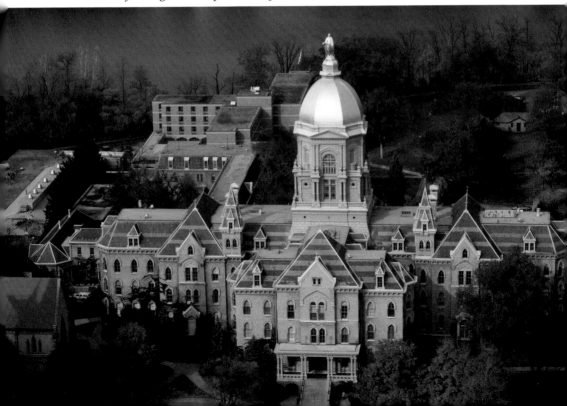

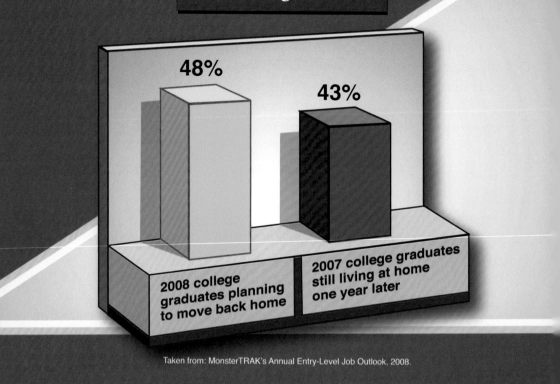

Boomerang Students

48%

2008 college graduates planning to move back home

43%

2007 college graduates still living at home one year later

Taken from: MonsterTRAK's Annual Entry-Level Job Outlook, 2008.

off-campus experience in fields such as "Urban Development and Social Change" and "Innovation and Entrepreneurship."

Programs such as these give undergraduates in the liberal arts the opportunity to step outside an academic framework and see how the subjects they are studying connect to life beyond college. Such programs also allow students to reflect on what their experiences have taught them about themselves and the world.

Those who have participated in such programs typically report that their off-campus activities helped them achieve a clearer sense of who they are, what they value, and where they want to go after graduation. The experience, they say, also adds to their understanding of the subjects they are studying. Employers and graduate programs tend to prefer students with experience in the fields in which they intend to work or to pursue advanced degrees.

Most colleges today advertise some sort of internship program. Only a limited number, however, have created structured, well-supported programs that help students find and prepare for the right placement, link that experience back to classroom work, and provide for reflection in a mentored setting.

It is important for applicants interested in a college's off-campus opportunities to ask how these programs are organized. Programs that are thoughtfully conceived, well-staffed, and embedded in the overall educational experience will contribute the most to their education.

College can be one life's richest experiences. While considering which college has the most beautiful campus or the highest ranking, however, families and students should remember that college is both an experience in itself and a building block of a total life structure. They should choose a college that takes this latter role seriously.

EVALUATING THE AUTHOR'S ARGUMENTS:

In this viewpoint Richard M. Freeland says students should choose colleges that help prepare them for life after graduation. Do you think this should be an important consideration in the choice of a college? If not, why? If so, how important a consideration should it be? What do you think the top five considerations for choosing a college should be?

Ivy League Colleges Have Advantages

Tim Lee

In the following viewpoint Tim Lee says that having an Ivy League degree offers advantages, particularly for some professions. The designation "Ivy League" refers to eight schools (Brown, Columbia, Cornell, Dartmouth, Harvard, Princeton, University of Pennsylvania, and Yale) located in the northeast which, with the exception of Cornell, were founded during the colonial period. All of the Ivy League universities place near the top in the *U.S. News & World Report* college rankings and are among the most generously endowed (supported with gifts of money) schools in the nation. Lee says that the primary benefits of attending an Ivy League school are related to having well-connected classmates and professors. Tim Lee is an adjunct scholar at the Cato Institute and a regular contributor to a variety of online publications.

"Where you went to school can matter quite a lot."

AS YOU READ, CONSIDER THE FOLLOWING QUESTIONS:

1. What kind of profession is Tim Lee in? Did he go to an Ivy League school?
2. According to the author, he is not surprised that studies have found little correlation between Ivy League attendance and what?
3. According to Lee, being a good journalist or policy analyst is largely a function of what?

Tim Lee, "Does It Matter Where You Went to School?" *Technology Liberation Front*, September 5, 2007. Reproduced by permission of the author.

As someone in a status-conscious profession who didn't go to an Ivy League school, I would like to believe that [Essayist] Paul Graham is right about this [it may not matter where you went to school]. But although I certainly think it's true that the value of an Ivy League education is often overstated, I don't think it's true that it doesn't matter where you went to college.

To get the obvious point out of the way first, I believe him that an Ivy League education won't make you any smarter. If you were smart when they accepted you, you'll be just as smart when you leave. And since to a first approximation career success is a function of intelligence and determination, neither of which an Ivy League college can impart, I'm not surprised that studies have found little correlation between Ivy League attendance and lifetime earnings.

FAST FACT

Harvard University, established in 1636 in Cambridge, Massachusetts, is the oldest U.S. university.

Ivy League schools, such as Yale, offer advantages in classroom environment and networking.

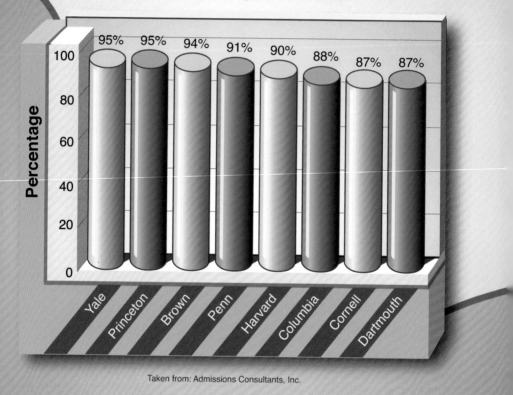

Ivy League Classmates Are Smart

Percent of students who were in the top 10 percent of their high school class.

Yale 95%
Princeton 95%
Brown 94%
Penn 91%
Harvard 90%
Columbia 88%
Cornell 87%
Dartmouth 87%

Percentage

Taken from: Admissions Consultants, Inc.

Classmates

However, I think an Ivy League institution offers two important advantages, both relating to who your classmates are. First, the intelligence of your classmates determines the pace of your classes. . . . Professors pace their classes to be understandable to the average student. If you're significantly smarter than the average student in a class, you're not going to learn as much as you could be learning, and if you're lazy and undisciplined, like I was at 19, you might get bored and stop showing up for class entirely.

Second, in most professions, who you know does matter. It matters more in some professions than others, of course, but there are hardly any professions in which it doesn't matter at all. Indeed, Graham himself has noted that one of the best ways to meet possible startup-founder-partners is to meet them in college. And although there are smart people at every college, on the margin there will certainly be more smart people at Ivy League schools than non-Ivies.

It matters even more in public policy (this might be largely a reflection of the fact that public policy isn't an especially meritocratic [based on skill] field, but I don't think that's the entire explanation). Being a good journalist, policy analyst, lawyer, lobbyist, etc. is largely a function of knowing a lot of people who are doing things related to what you're doing, preferably in prominent positions. If I've got a question on education policy, for example, it's helpful to have in my rolodex [address book] a friend who works on education policy. People who go to Ivy League schools are likely to have a larger number of people in positions of power and influence than people who go to non-Ivies.

Who You Know

I would note that at least from an outsider's perspective, academia seems to be a bit of a special case in the sense that who your professors were actually does matter. Going to a good school for a PhD allows you to develop relationships with people whose recommendations will carry more weight on the academic job market. This seems to be the same mechanism that makes going to a good law school important to getting good clerkships, which in turn is a major qualification for being a law professor or judge. If you aspire to a profession in which a limited number of slots are doled out . . . by existing elites, where you went to school can matter quite a lot.

> **EVALUATING THE AUTHOR'S ARGUMENTS:**
>
> Explain how, as Tim Lee asserts, having an Ivy League education can help the student who endeavors to be a lawyer. Do you think that going to an Ivy League school has advantages if you want to be an elementary school teacher? Explain.

Small Liberal Arts Colleges Are Better than Large Universities

Loren Pope

"The good small liberal arts college will give you the best and most challenging education."

In the following viewpoint Loren Pope argues that small colleges are better than large universities. Pope calls four-year liberal arts colleges with student bodies of around three thousand students or fewer "small good colleges." He says students at these colleges learn more and have better experiences than students at universities. Pope says students can get lost in large universities and rarely get to know their professors. On the other hand, says Pope, at "small good colleges" students have a sense of community, classes are small, and students get to know and work with their professors. Pope provides testimonials from students and parents who attended small good colleges, or wish they would have. Pope has been involved in higher education for more than fifty years. He was the education editor at the *New York Times*, an

Loren Pope, *Looking Beyond the Ivy League.* New York, NY: Penguin Books, 2007. Copyright © Loren Pope, 1990, 1995, 2007. All rights reserved. Reprinted by permission of Ann Rittenberg Literary Agency.

administrator at Oakland University in Michigan, a college counselor, and the author of several college guides.

AS YOU READ, CONSIDER THE FOLLOWING QUESTIONS:
1. According to Pope, who said that liberal education in large universities is in ruins?
2. Why does Pope say that student interaction with classmates and teachers outside of the classroom—what he calls "cross-fertilization and making connections"—is important?
3. What did a Duke professor tell Pope about how hard you have work to get a B at Duke or other elite schools? What type of college did the Duke professor's daughter attend?

It is nonsense to think that bigger is better, especially in education. The good small liberal arts college will give you the best and most challenging education. It also will make you a better person, a more independent and creative thinker than the [large] university. The small college produces the pioneers and risk takers who will prosper in the new world. At the small college you will make long-lasting friendships with your professors. The university fails on all these counts. In fact, such things are not on its agenda; it thinks it has bigger fish to fry. . . .

After *Sputnik*, federal dollars for research to catch up with the Russians changed the universities into research institutes. By now, . . . their commitment to Mammon [a false god of riches and greed] is so binding that a noted Princeton scholar, Stanley N. Katz, president emeritus of the American Council of Learned Societies, has warned that liberal education in them "is a project in ruins" that threatens "the vitality" of American democracy. They're "uncomfortable with values," and values are central to the good small college. His indictment includes not only the Ivies and their clones but scores of wannabees.

Nevertheless, Dr. Katz says, "liberal education is alive and well in the small colleges." "Small" comes in many sizes, from Marlboro's 300 to St. Olaf's or Hope's 3,200. But student bodies much larger than that dilute the sense of community.

Small Colleges Offer Collaboration, Not Competition

There is no magic curriculum, program, or method, for the good small colleges do many different things. The magic lies in how they do it. Students and professors collaborate rather than compete. Discussion of values is emphasized. Students are heavily involved in their own education; they work with each other and with their teachers. It is collaborative, not competitive. They coauthor research papers or books with their teachers and so are a big step ahead in graduate school and in many jobs. They are hiking or dinner companions or intramural teammates, and in these relaxed occasions get insights from bright minds across the spectrum of scholarship. This is cross-fertilization and making connections. It is part of the students' search to find themselves, and may be as or more important than what happens in the classroom. It is just what the adolescent mind needs at this stage. If a student feels the need, he can specialize later, and more profitably, when he's more mature. He may come to college expecting a career in biology or international relations and wind up as a music or physics major. This is the kind of intellectual stimulus the small college offers, as Dr. Sam Shulman points out in his book *Old Main*, an examination of a dozen small colleges.

FAST FACT

Three percent of bachelor degrees granted in the 2005–2006 academic year in the United States were in liberal arts and sciences, general studies, or humanities.

A vital ingredient that makes for far better teachers is that the good small college changes professors' lives, too. At college after college across the country, faculty members would give me variations of what a professor at Hendrix said: "I came here expecting to stay a few years and move on to a research university, but now you couldn't blast me out of here." They also would say that nowhere else had they experienced such collegiality, lack of politics and infighting, or freedom to disagree and remain friends. Or, as a professor who'd had tenure at Vanderbilt said, "My smallest class there was seventy-five. I wanted to be with students and talk with them." Such avowals reflect the secret ingredient that helps

Like this small undergraduate math class at Williams College in Massachusetts, small liberal arts colleges offer a curriculum where students and faculty collaborate rather than compete.

work the magic of the good small college that the university turns its nose up at.

Universities More Concerned About Research

The university offers a different kind of depth in one field and on the graduate level. It is an aggregate of scholars whose focus is on research to increase knowledge and on graduate students. Undergraduates are nuisances that subsidize research and get short shrift. They may never have a conversation with a professor, or even write a paper.

The intellectual awakening in the small college is passionately voiced for uncounted thousands in other schools in the words of a

Hiram junior: "Many catalytic things have happened to me. These are incredible people. They love to teach. We have a mentor relationship. They are always making cross-connections from one area or discipline to another. They are always encouraging, pushing me to do better. There is so much pressure, so many responsibilities it forces you to keep going. They say 'this might be a publishable paper'. One would like to come back here to teach—or to one like it."

Her testimonial reminded me of a Hiram freshman and client, years earlier, who'd written his mother: "I've never had to work so hard in all my life! This place is great!" Both of these comments are echoed in the Ten Years Later sections at the end of the college profiles in the second edition of *Colleges That Change Lives* [an educational guide authored by Pope, which profiles Pope's top 40 choices for liberal arts colleges], as well as in comments I've received from clients over a period of nearly forty years. In fact, one girl wrote on the cover of her graduation invitation: "Loren, Kalamazoo really did change my life!"

Bigger Is Not Better

But from clients who've gone to an Ivy or Ivy clone (often against my advice), I've never heard such a testimonial. One client told me on a visit there, "It's hard to be humble at Amherst." A mother called to report her disappointed daughter had written, "Michigan is everything Mr. Pope said it was and I'm going to transfer." A junior in Michigan's honors program, like many at other universities, couldn't get a single needed class in her major. As a girl who came to me after a year at the University of Florida said, "They may have two thousand courses, but try to get in one; you're bound to get screwed."

And a dentist friend and his wife persuaded their son to transfer from Washington University in St. Louis, a first-rate school, to the University of Wisconsin because it was bigger and had more facilities, and therefore would be a better entrée into medical school. They were wrong. Wisconsin rejected him, but the medical school admission director at Washington U. told me they would have taken him because he was a known commodity, and the profs who gave him recommendations were known to the medical school admissions

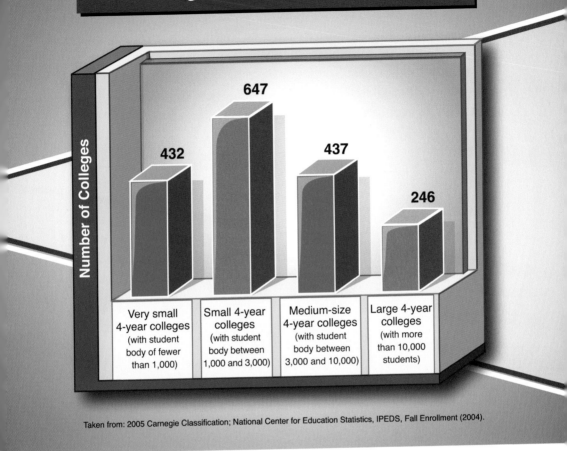

Most Colleges Have Smaller Student Bodies

Number of Colleges

| Very small 4-year colleges (with student body of fewer than 1,000) | Small 4-year colleges (with student body between 1,000 and 3,000) | Medium-size 4-year colleges (with student body between 3,000 and 10,000) | Large 4-year colleges (with more than 10,000 students) |
| 432 | 647 | 437 | 246 |

Taken from: 2005 Carnegie Classification; National Center for Education Statistics, IPEDS, Fall Enrollment (2004).

committee. He finally got the last-gasp acceptance at another medical school.

Good Small Colleges Are the Best

Many a parent has written to say they wish they'd had as good experiences as their kids who'd gone to good small colleges. One father told me, "I didn't know what a lousy experience I'd had at the University of Texas until I read your books." A Duke professor, who'd written an article saying "learning is optional" there, told me at the time, "You don't have to do any work to get a B here, and I think the same thing is true at other elite schools." His daughter went to a good small college.

During my counseling career, faculty members from Harvard, MIT, Johns Hopkins, Michigan, Wisconsin, Georgetown, George Washington, American, Maryland, West Virginia, Duke, North Carolina, and others I don't recall brought their children to me, expecting them to go to a small college.

And finally, the small colleges have been outperforming the big ones in producing America's future scientists, scholars, and other contributors ever since record-keeping began in 1920.

EVALUATING THE AUTHOR'S ARGUMENTS:

What are the reasons Loren Pope gives for saying that small good colleges are better than large universities? What does Pope say about Ivy League colleges in this viewpoint?

Public Universities Have Advantages

GoCollege.com

"Public and state universities have many benefits over their private counterparts."

In the following viewpoint GoCollege.com asserts that public colleges have many benefits. Public colleges receive most of their operating money from state and federal governments as opposed to private colleges that receive most of their money from private donors. According to GoCollege.com, one of the primary benefits of public colleges is that they can charge much lower tuition, particularly to students hailing from the same state as the college. According to GoCollege.com, other benefits of public colleges include diversity and a competitive environment. GoCollege .com is a Web site offering helpful information for current and prospective college students.

AS YOU READ, CONSIDER THE FOLLOWING QUESTIONS:
1. According to GoCollege.com, why are all students regardless of race, religion, gender sexual orientation, or any other characteristic eligible for admission to public universities?
2. What is the reason that student residents of any state often receive deeply discounted tuitions at in-state universities, as stated by the author?
3. According to GoCollege.com, what are the disadvantages of public universities?

"Public & State Universities," GoCollege.com, accessed July 16, 2008. Reproduced by permission.

D
o you prefer public or private, large or small colleges and universities? It's a choice you'll have to make when considering college. There are distinct differences between public and private universities beyond the obvious size of student body.

Public or state-funded universities operate in whole or in part on state or federal funds. This means all students regardless of race, religion, sex, sexual orientation or any other differentiating characteristic are eligible for admission. Conversely, private institutions may make exemptions, such as women-only campuses, or men-only, and religious schools and seminaries.

One of the advantages of big public universities, like the University of Michigan, is more affordable tuition rates.

The Benefits of Public and State Universities

Public and state universities have many benefits over their private counterparts.

Since the state or federal government provides operating funds for a public university most offer much more affordable tuitions across the board than do private colleges and universities. Student residents of any state often receive deeply discounted tuitions at in-state universities as opposed to out of state. Reason? Keeps students living and working within the state—it's economics.

Costs for room and board at a private university can be quite heady for average, middle-income students.

Some of the larger public universities in the U.S. are also home to state-of-the-art research facilities, science and medical labs, teaching hospitals, and libraries.

FAST FACT

Rhode Island has the fewest number of four-year public colleges (3) while California has the most four-year public colleges (144).

In such institutions students discover enclaves of world-renowned professors and have the opportunity to learn at their side, even participate in cutting-edge technological projects.

How do large public universities have all this in comparison to smaller universities and colleges? Large publicly funded universities also maintain quite lucrative financial coffers in addition to the public funds. This kind of financial leverage gives them the muscle to build and expand with the best facilities possible.

Smaller private institutions work very hard to attract a wide variety of students, but large universities manage more easily due to their visibility, affordability and resources. This innate diversity theoretically offers a deeper level of educational opportunity. Students may work collaboratively with others from different backgrounds, cultures, and by doing so rewrite the collective knowledge base.

Large public universities tend to foster and encourage competition. When students consistently try to best their peers the institution only grows stronger. Research reaches new levels, students graduate with top grades and credentials, all of which help build a school's selectivity level.

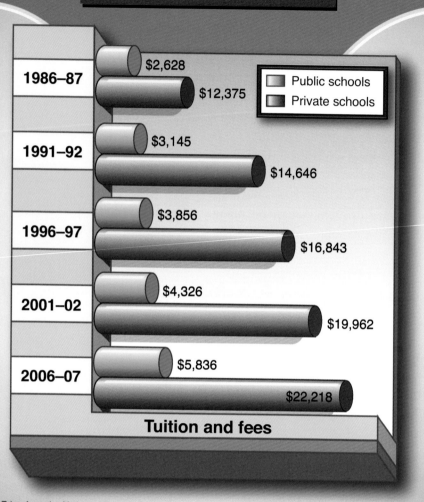

Public Schools Cost Less

	Public schools	Private schools
1986–87	$2,628	$12,375
1991–92	$3,145	$14,646
1996–97	$3,856	$16,843
2001–02	$4,326	$19,962
2006–07	$5,836	$22,218

Tuition and fees

Taken from: Jay Mathews, "Spikes in College Price Tags Not So Sharp," *Washington Post*, October 25, 2006.

Some Disadvantages

Large public universities can be vibrant educational hubs, but for the wrong student they can also spell disaster.

- Students timid about their academics may become lost in the shuffle and fail to thrive on a large campus.
- Many lower level classes are taught by doctoral students who spend time as professors' assistants.
- Much harder to get personal attention from staff or faculty when needed.

Applying for Admission to a Public University

The admissions process associated with a large university is much less navigable than one on a small private campus. When you apply there is no room for error and oversight and admissions personnel have little time for handholding. Make mistakes on your application and it's going in the trash. To avoid this make sure your application is complete, on time or early and has all the required documentation attached.

EVALUATING THE AUTHORS' ARGUMENTS:

In this viewpoint GoCollege.com discusses the advantages and disadvantages of large public universities. In the previous viewpoint, Loren Pope touts the benefits of small good colleges. After reading the two viewpoints, which type of college would *you* like to attend and why?

Chapter 3

What Factors Impact a Student's Ability to Attend College?

Many factors will impact students in their search for a college that meets their needs.

It Costs Too Much Money to Go to College

"*Relative to other sectors of the economy, universities are becoming less efficient, less productive, and, consequently, most costly.*"

Richard Vedder

In the following viewpoint Richard Vedder argues that college is too expensive and a potential waste of money. Vedder challenges conventional beliefs that college makes people more productive and therefore is a good investment. Vedder believes colleges would cost less and be a better investment if they were run more efficiently and more like a "business." Vedder is an economics professor at Ohio University and the director of the Center for College Affordability, a nonprofit research center dedicated to research on the issues of rising costs and stagnant efficiency in higher education.

AS YOU READ, CONSIDER THE FOLLOWING QUESTIONS:
1. According to Vedder, devoting more subsidies to colleges will not necessarily lower tuition and increase the number of college graduates. He points out that in one statistical exercise his student assistants found that for each state-appropriated dollar, tuition was only lowered by how many cents?

Richard Vedder, *Over Invested and Over Priced*. Washington, DC: Center for College Affordability and Productivity, 2007. Reproduced by permission.

2. According to Vedder, for most sectors of the economy, productivity increases over time. However, this is not true for colleges and universities. According to Vedder, what reason will defenders of universities give for the lack of increased productivity for colleges and universities?
3. According to Vedder, does it cost more to educate graduate students or undergraduate students? Who pays more tuition, graduate students or undergraduate students, as stated by the author?

The prevailing view among leaders in the university community is that America is not investing enough in higher education. A recent survey of the American economy by the Organization for Economic Cooperation and Development (OECD) echoed that concern. After all, college graduates are dramatically more productive than those without higher education preparation, and America is falling behind other nations in the proportion of the adult population with college degrees. National competitiveness and economic well-being are at risk, or so it is argued.

The conventional wisdom downplays the concerns about rising costs, particularly soaring tuition fees. One argument is that the cost explosion is an illusion: "net tuition fees" (sticker tuition prices minus scholarship aid and loans) have risen less dramatically than gross tuition fees (published rates). Americans think college costs are greater than they really are. Besides, the rate of return of a university education remains high, since the earnings differential associated with college has risen over the past several decades in tandem with fees, maintaining a high return on the financial investment.

Yet I think most of these arguments are flawed, even downright wrong. An excellent case can be made that we are *over invested* in universities, that too many students attend school, that much of our investment is wasted. Moreover, the rise in costs—to society, to taxpayers, and especially to consumers—is excessive, and has been made more so by well meaning but inappropriate public policies. The law of unintended consequences looms large in any discussion of America's colleges and universities.

Reviewing Conventional Wisdom

Before elaborating on the claim that America actually over invests in higher education and that costs are rising at an economic unjustifiably rapid rate, let us review some evidence promoting the conventional wisdom. The evidence shows that the proportion of adult Americans with college degrees is rising, but far less rapidly than in many other industrialized lands. As a consequence, the United States no longer leads the world in this regard. Moreover, many other countries seem to be expanding the proportion of the population with college degrees rapidly, which is far less true in the U.S., where participation in university education by some measures is rising very slowly, if at all.

This matters, conventional wisdom holds, because college graduates are vastly more productive than non-college graduates. For example, data from the 2006 Current Population Survey show that in 2005 full-time year-round workers with bachelor's degrees on average earned over 76 percent more than comparable workers with only high school diplomas. Economists agree that wages and salaries are very highly correlated with productivity. . . . Paying for a college education is investing in human capital. . . .

For most, the argument goes, college is a good investment. In 2005, the average earnings of full-time year-round workers with bachelor's degrees, $65,281, were $27,251 higher than for comparable workers with high school diplomas. The discounted present value of that lifetime earnings differential (from 35–40 years of working), is several hundred thousand dollars, vastly more than the cost of four years of higher education, even allowing for the loss of income from not working a job while attending college.

Problems with the Conventional Wisdom

Yet there are two huge problems with the conventional wisdom. First, devoting more subsidies to higher education does not necessarily mean the number of college graduates will increase, as is assumed by the advocates of greater governmental appropriations. At the margin, newly appropriated funds may go for a variety of non-instructional purposes—administrative personnel, student services, intercollegiate athletics, research, higher compensation levels for key personnel, etc. In one statistical exercise, my student assistants at the Center for

College Affordability and Productivity (CCAP) estimated that historically, each one dollar of added state appropriations per student leads to only 30 cents in lower tuition per student at state universities. Most of the incremental appropriations lead to higher spending instead of lower tuition fees that would stimulate new enrollments. Indeed, at many state universities with enrollment ceilings, higher appropriations have no enrollment effects whatsoever. Prestige is gained by *denying* students access. In economics jargon, the supply is perfectly inelastic. . . .

Productivity of College Grads Not Totally About College

There is a second problem with the conventional wisdom. While it is true that college graduates are more productive than those not attending college, it is unclear that most of that higher productivity has anything to do with going to college. College graduates, on average, are more intelligent, more motivated, more disciplined, and more honest than non-college graduates. As Richard Herrnstein and Charles Murray famously and controversially noted in *The Bell Curve*, the average IQ of college graduates is notably higher than that of their non-collegiate counterparts. Relatively uneducated persons have higher crime rates (a measure of unreliability and untrustworthiness) than college trained counterparts.

When employers hire a college graduate and pay a relatively good salary to that person, are they primarily renting use of the skills the student acquired in college, or are they renting qualities largely acquired before college—maturity, discipline, intelligence, honesty? The answer, of course, is that some employers do buy college-generated skills— knowledge of accounting, advanced engineering skills, etc.—but a large part of what they buy are skills and traits not directly related to the college experience. It is wrong to attribute the high school/college earnings differential solely or even predominantly to things "taught" in college. . . .

Why Are Universities Overpriced?

It takes more resources today to educate a postsecondary student than a generation ago. That is not true for most goods and services, where productivity advances assisted by capital formation and technologi-

College graduates have average annual earnings of $65,281 as opposed to the $27,251 earnings by those with just a high school diploma.

cal advances have lowered the resources needed to produce a single unit of output. Relative to other sectors of the economy, universities are becoming less efficient, less productive, and, consequently, most costly.

Defenders of universities will say a major reason for this is the so-called Baumol Effect, named after economist William Baumol. Baumol correctly observed that in the fine arts, the productivity of employees cannot be increased, so the relative costs of providing services rises. It takes the same number of actors and actresses to perform *Medea* today as it did when Euripides wrote and produced it more than 2,400 years ago. A modern day painter, even if capable, would take as long as Da Vinci to paint the *Mona Lisa*. In the arts, there are very limited opportunities for capital-labor substitution, for using cost-saving techniques, etc.

Is the same thing true of universities? It is true that much of teaching *as it is done today* is like theater, with an "actor" (the professor) performing a monologue to an audience of students. But does it have to be done that way? Could not enormous savings be realized by expanding audiences via electronic means, by using taped lectures on multiple occasions, or by utilizing interactive computerized learning approaches in survey courses? A number of for-profit providers are showing that these techniques do have considerable promise, yet they are still used only sparingly in higher education. I do not think it is much of an exaggeration to say that, with the possible exception of prostitution, teaching is the only profession that has had absolutely no productivity advance in the 2,400 years since Socrates taught the youth of Athens. . . .

FAST FACT

For the 2006–2007 academic year, college tuition at public and private schools was more than double what it was in 1990, according to the U.S. Census Bureau.

Twelve Reasons for Rising Prices

I would argue that the environment in which universities operate contributes mightily to the observed cost explosion. Universities behave differently than most other institutions in American society. In giving them enormous autonomy and independence in order to protect the free flow of ideas, we have created highly inefficient institutions that are anti-innovative and increasingly costly. Twelve words or phrases sum up the cause of most of the problem, and solving the cost explosion involves modifying these twelve sometimes overlapping points. A brief discussion of each follows.

1. Third Party Payments

The people paying a majority of the bills in higher education are not the users of higher education services. When someone else is paying the bills, consumers are less conscious of cost considerations, and that in turn leads to some distortion and inefficient use of inputs used to produce higher education services. It is not a coincidence that the two big components of the Consumer Price Index with greatest price increases—health care and higher education fees—both have large third party payments.

2. Non-Profit

More than 95 percent of the resources in higher education are spent at non-profit institutions. Where profits exist, they signal how resources should be allocated: when profits are high, resources move into an activity; when they are low, resources exit it. The critical signaling role of profits is absent from higher education, excepting the small but robust for-profit sector. . . .

3. Bottom Line
Profits are the bottom line of competitive market business enterprises, and they are signaling devices that inform and direct decisions. The lack of a bottom line in higher education means it is hard to tell if schools are meeting goals, and what the goals are. Did Stanford have a good year in 2006? Who knows? Firms like *U.S. News & World Report* try to create a non-market bottom line, often based on dubious measures (e.g., inputs used instead of outputs). Instead of cutting costs to increase profits, colleges often enhance costs to buy things (good students, more faculty) that improve magazine rankings, not knowing if it truly improves teaching and research. . . .

4. Resource Rigidities
Many of the costs in higher education are fixed, making colleges somewhat like public utilities. Tenure, designed to enhance academic freedom, makes it difficult to reallocate faculty resources to alternative uses. Universities are often slow to rapidly increase instruction where employment demand is soaring, and also slow to reduce or eliminate costly programs no longer in much demand. The lack of incentives to meet consumer demands and cut costs means change often comes too slowly and tepidly. . . .

5. Barriers to Entry and Restraints on Competition
For-profit educational entrepreneurs frequently complain that accreditation raises costs and impedes entry of new institutions. Accreditation procedures can lead universities to act like cartels, agreeing to the rules of the game for operation, excluding newcomers with innovative ideas and sometimes a better product at a lower price. . . .

6. Public Support and Control
The fact that most third party support for higher education comes from governments means that higher education is to some extent politicized. Universities must conform to numerous rules in order to qualify for government grants. State colleges and universities often face added restrictions—the tuition they can charge, the salaries they

can pay, the composition of their governing board, etc.—that have deleterious effects. Higher education has faced funding stagnation from governments because of politically more compelling competing needs, such as Medicaid.

7. Price Discrimination

Universities are adroit at charging whatever the traffic will bear, making wealthy students without unusual distinction pay high tuition fees, but giving discounts to persons on the basis of need, but also on the basis of special skills (extremely high levels of intelligence, high competence in throwing or catching balls) or racial/ethnic/gender status. Price discrimination has grown, and some of the financing of institutional financial aid has come from aggressive increases in sticker prices. Only universities do not tell consumers the price they have to pay for a service until they have given intimate financial and personal information.

8. Rent-Seeking

Economists use the term "economic rent" to refer to payments made that have no impact on economic activity. Compensation of employees beyond what market forces dictate is common in higher education. There is a strong correlation, for example, between federal research grants and salaries of senior professors. Many persons obtain grants to do what they would have done anyway without the grants, raising the total cost of higher education.

9. Cross Subsidization

It costs vastly more to educate graduate students than undergraduate students, but they typically pay less (after financial aid) in tuition, meaning non-tuition revenues subsidize them vastly more than undergraduates. Schools have reduced teaching loads over the years to allow for more research but still expect students to pick up much of the cost. At some schools tuition fees significantly exceed the direct instructional costs for undergraduates.

10. Ownership

Who owns the universities? Who has property rights? Lots of groups *think* they own institutions—the trustees (who typically have nominal ownership control), the faculty, the alumni, state government

Colleges Are Getting More Money but Are Spending Less on Student Instruction

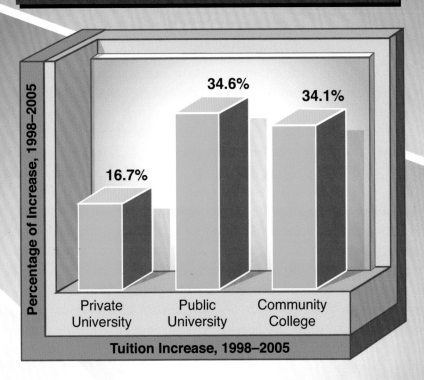

Percentage of Increase, 1998–2005

16.7%

34.6%

34.1%

Private University

Public University

Community College

Tuition Increase, 1998–2005

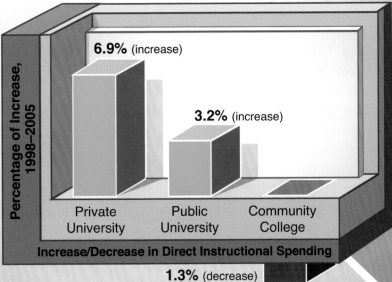

Percentage of Increase, 1998–2005

6.9% (increase)

3.2% (increase)

Private University

Public University

Community College

Increase/Decrease in Direct Instructional Spending

1.3% (decrease)

Taken from: Mary Beth Marklein, "Value of College Tuition Called into Question," *USA Today*, May 1, 2008. Delta Cost Project, based on U.S. Education Department Data.

officials, sometimes even students. This causes turf wars and unproductive wastage of resources: for example, the chemistry department claims a building belongs to it, even though it might be wiser to use some of the space for other needs.

11. Governance
A closely related issue to ownership is governance. Who runs universities? Often decisions are made not by a strong chief executive but by committees, leading to vast resources going into decision-making and to cautious, non-innovative policies. Universities are about the only place where subordinates (e.g., faculty) often select their own bosses (e.g. deans or even university presidents). This leads to blurred lines of authority, divided leadership, and high administrative costs.

12. Information
Partly because of a lack of performance indicators, colleges do not tell prospective customers what the "value added" is for attending their institutions. They often do not readily provide useful data: What percent of the students graduate in four years? How many kids are assaulted or robbed each year? What percent of university revenues go for instruction? This knowledge deficiency often leads to poorly informed consumers making bad decisions as to the appropriate institution to attend.

What Should We Do?
In deciding what to do, it must be kept in mind that universities are relatively inefficient institutions partly sheltered from the discipline of the market—a discipline that provides incentives for cost reductions, product improvement, and innovation. What entrepreneur Charles Koch calls "market based management" needs to be more vigorously introduced into the academy.

Part of the move to more market-based management is a weaning of universities from heavy government support. My research suggests that support should become more limited and selective—perhaps eliminating student loans for affluent students, for example, or restricting assistance for schools with low graduation rates. Probably we should abandon institutional subsidization altogether, instead giving needy, well performing students vouchers, enhancing consumer market power; and forcing schools to be more attentive to student needs. Policy makers should use cost-benefit calculations to evaluate their spending on universities and learn more about what goes on at them.

As to reducing prices, obviously the solution involves modifying some or all of the twelve points mentioned above. Lower third party payments, revisit contractual arrangements that cause resource rigidities, encourage market-oriented for-profit schools with a bottom line, ease accreditation barriers, etc. . . .

The high school/college earnings differential may have stopped growing, so the investment return to college will start falling unless costs are contained. Our colleges and universities were not created in a day, nor will reform and change come easily. But we must begin the process if higher education is going to better promote the advance of our civilization and our material prosperity.

EVALUATING THE AUTHOR'S ARGUMENTS:

In this viewpoint Richard Vedder contends that colleges are very inefficient "businesses," and that is why they cost so much. What examples does Vedder use to support his contention that colleges are inefficient?

There Are Reasons for High College Tuition

Paul Marthers

"*Colleges and universities . . . have let themselves get defined as money-driven, price-gouging wealth-accumulating firms rather than as cathedrals of learning.*"

In the following viewpoint Paul Marthers asserts that colleges need to justify their costs and tell their own unique stories in order to battle back against those who portray them as inefficient and overpriced. According to Marthers, there are reasons why college tuitions are high, and colleges need to point this out to the public. Marthers says that Reed College has successfully told its story—at Reed a student obtains a handcrafted education—and justified its tuition, and he recommends that other colleges start crafting their own narratives. Marthers is dean of admission at Reed College, a private liberal arts college located in Portland, Oregon.

AS YOU READ, CONSIDER THE FOLLOWING QUESTIONS:

1. According to Marthers, what is the impact of putting too much emphasis on college as a commodity? How do colleges themselves encourage this kind of thinking?

Paul Marthers, "In Need of a Persuasive Story," *Inside Higher Ed,* January 24, 2008. Reproduced by permission.

2. According to the author, how should colleges react when politicians rail about passing on nonacademic costs to students in their tuition bill?
3. What will the U.S. Congress's next Higher Education Act call for colleges to do, according to Marthers?

L ate last year [2007] I was in Washington, D.C., listening to government officials and policy analysts discuss the state of higher education in America. The tone of those conversations, as has been the case since the advent of the Spellings Commission, was troubling. I left with the clear impression that there is widespread distrust of colleges and universities in Washington on both sides of the political aisle.

That means suspicion of higher education is not a partisan issue and that the era of accountability and cost sensitivity will not end when the Bush administration leaves town. Key public officials like Massachusetts Sen. Edward Kennedy and California Rep. Howard P. (Buck) McKeon will probably continue to rail about rising college costs. And the higher education sector will probably continue to be hampered by its inability to tell a believable story about why tuitions keep increasing at rates higher than inflation.

Suspicion, Distrust, and Unflattering Stories

To a certain degree, suspicion and distrust of colleges and universities are problems of the higher education sector's own making. College and university leaders, most of whom were faculty members at some point, have the professor's reflex against simplified explanations. Professorial skepticism toward neat, tidy, simple (but often inaccurate) answers is understandable and admirable. But politicians and reporters like to hear coherent and compelling narratives that are easy to understand and easy to retell to their constituents and readers. Higher education has often failed to grasp this. And it shows in the explanations higher education gives about the rising cost issue: They are all too often defensive or obfuscating [confusing]—leaving the public scratching its head in perplexity.

The stories being told in Washington about higher education, as everyone working at a college or university knows, are not flattering.

The dominant stories coming from the mouths of politicians and the pens of reporters portray America's colleges and universities in an arms race to out-compete each other on rankings, wealth, prestige, student diversity, scholarships and financial aid, faculty compensation, teaching loads, and non-academic facilities. College professors are depicted as disinterested in students and eager to have decreased teaching responsibilities. College administrators are pilloried as over-paid, unnecessary bureaucrats—although, ironically, government intervention nearly always requires colleges to hire more administrators to comply with the reporting requirements imposed by legislators. And who hasn't read or heard stories of dormitories overbuilt in the image of four-star luxury hotels or of million dollar-climbing walls? Tales of the latter have become the stuff of urban legend.

Critics Say Colleges Should Be Run Like Businesses

The dominant meme [cultural idea] describes American colleges and universities as institutions driven by their own self-interest rather than by the interests of students or of society. Lost in the debate is any sense of the public's interest in anything other than the politics of resentment, which builds its persuasive case through portrayals of colleges and universities as bloated, elitist, inefficient, unworthy of tax payer support, and lacking the ethical high ground. If only colleges and universities were run like a business goes a common critique that warms the hearts of the for-profit higher education sector and its key Congressional supporters like Ohio Rep. John Boehner. Applying business principles is the panacea according to this simplistic but seductive narrative that has put colleges and universities on the defensive since the beginning of the Reagan administration.

Magazine and newspaper articles increasingly depict a college education in business terms, as a consumer good to be purchased. Customers (students and their parents) are encouraged to seek the best deal, to bargain, to devise strategies to pay the lowest price for the highest quality. The ubiquitous so-called merit scholarship, which in most cases is nothing more than a price discount to lure another customer, makes it nearly impossible for any five parents with children at the same college to know how much the others are paying. The situation is akin to the airline industry where invariably no two seats on the same plane are sold for the same amount.

The emphasis on cost to the paying customer casts a college education squarely in the realm of commodity. And to be sure, there has always been an inherent commodity aspect to the experience of getting a college education. Most American colleges have never been free, and historically most students have entered college seeking upward economic and social mobility. But too much emphasis on college as commodity, voiced by students or by colleges, corrupts higher education, leading colleges and universities to be seen primarily as businesses churning out product rather than as places that inspire, enlighten, and uplift society. Even the colleges themselves have encouraged this kind of thinking to justify why students and parents should be willing to pay the rising cost of college—as institutions often cite studies showing a $1 million lifetime earnings advantage for college graduates over non-college graduates.

FAST FACT

In the 2004–2005 academic year, public four-year colleges spent on average $23,353 to educate each student, while private nonprofit four-year colleges spent on average $38,472 per student, according to the National Center on Education Statistics.

Colleges Need to Tell Their Stories

On the issue of rising tuitions, colleges and universities, as they have exuberantly embraced marketplace paradigms, have let themselves get defined as money-driven, price-gouging wealth-accumulating firms rather than as cathedrals of learning. This has happened because colleges and universities have not been bold in telling their collective story. Instead, colleges and universities have let themselves end up in the defensive position of rebutting the unflattering stories and simplistic caricatures about why college costs so much. Those stories and caricatures, when left unchecked, undermine the public's trust in higher education.

There are potential opportunities for colleges and universities to begin shaping the story from within higher education rather than simply reacting to stories from without. But the first step is to craft accurate, uncomplicated, and believable narratives.

President George W. Bush signs the College Accessibility and Access Act aimed at making college more affordable for low-income students.

Small Liberal Arts Schools Like Artisans' Workshops

The case for the small liberal arts college offers one starting point. Providing an education at a small liberal arts college is a highly individualized process. The liberal arts college classroom is more akin to an artisan's workshop or an artist's studio than to a factory floor or an assembly line. If higher education must be forced to adopt the language of the business transaction, then perhaps the small liberal arts college must make the case, as Reed College's President Colin Diver often has, that consumers always pay higher prices for, and are more willing to make sacrifices to afford, handcrafted goods in comparison to mass-produced goods. Diver's argument is compelling because it is self-evident to most consumers that craftsmanship is synonymous with quality.

Nor is it a stretch to claim that a liberal arts education is the product of craftsmanship, the result of a slow, labor-intensive process that produces individually unique student learners whose lives have been transformed for the better by four years at the institution. One enduring image of the small college education has the eminent 19th century Williams College professor Mark Hopkins on one end of a log and a student on the other end. The Hopkins image came to symbolize the intimate small college transmission of knowledge from sage to student.

Colleges That Change Lives, by the former *New York Times* education editor Loren Pope, has garnered a following due to its message that small costly private colleges, like Earlham and Reed, perform a kind of educational alchemy not easily broken down into bottom-line terms but somehow are able to deliver on the promise of the book's title. Pope's book has drawn attention to 40 colleges that are not the household names invoked by politicians trying to make hay out of critiques of higher education. Yet Pope's 40 colleges are collectively one example of the kind of compelling story that, if told more often, might help private higher education regain the public's trust.

Justify Costs with Straight Talk

When justifying the high cost of college, is it enough to assert, as countless presidents of private liberal arts colleges have, that the actual production costs of educating a student are sometimes double the tuition charge? I do not think so. In fact, I suspect that the public hears such arguments and imagines that higher education is wasteful. After all, what product costs twice as much to produce as its sale price? What firm survives producing such a product? Discerning consumers wonder how much of that double-the-sticker-price true cost pays for the hidden costs of fund raising, public relations, student recruiting, and athletic programs; that is, enterprises not regarded as being at the core of most colleges and universities, but precisely the areas that many people immediately associate with the runaway cost of higher education.

Rather than change the subject when politicians rail about the so-called non-academic costs that get passed on to students in the tuition bill, colleges need to hit the issue head on. Straight talk about non-core costs might be appealing to the public and disarming to higher education's critics. There are potentially persuasive ways to justify the non-academic costs of running a college or university. For example, why not just assert that the expenses incurred by college fund-raising and endowment management enterprises are examples of how colleges gather non-tuition revenues to keep their tuitions from rising even higher? College leaders can say with authority that those revenue-chasing expenditures, rather than being cited in the cost of educating a student, might more appropriately be charged off against the endowment and fund raising returns. The public might then understand that, without the marginal dollars netted through fund raising and endowment returns, tuitions would be much higher.

Similarly, colleges can justify their public relations and recruiting expenditures as the price of bringing in quality students and faculty as well as the price of enhancing the perceived value of the degree the student will earn. Finally, colleges can argue that they provide their students a unique lifetime affiliation that accrues benefit long after the last tuition check gets paid. How many firms can say that about their product?

And if none of those arguments work, colleges can do what they have been loath to; that is, point to the students and parents in the consuming public and say, in the words of an old Toyota commercial, "you asked for it, you got it." That's right. College tuitions have gone up because students and their parents expect more from the college experience than ever. Meeting those expectations does not happen when institutions run in place to hold down costs. To get less expensive colleges, the public will have to accept less expansive college degree programs and facilities. There is no evidence that the public is willing to do so; nor should it. In any case, both are points that higher education needs to make early and often.

Candor and transparency about the costs they charge is something colleges and universities will have to practice soon enough as Congressional interest in a "College Access and Affordability Act" has made it into the next reauthorization of the Higher Education Act (HEA). The next HEA will call for colleges to provide students and their parents with more transparent and detailed explanations of the costs they charge. The emphasis on explaining and justifying costs will, in the hopes of some members of Congress, influence colleges to hold down future tuition increases. . . .

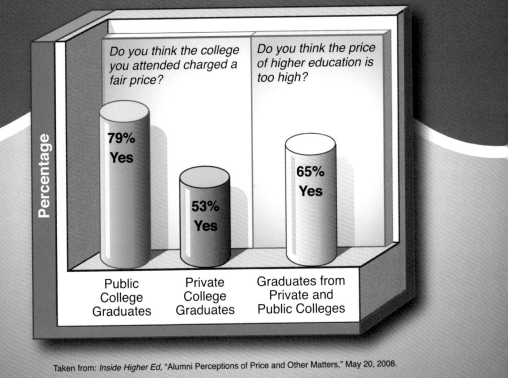

College Alumni Mostly Think the Price They Paid for College Is Fair

One thousand college graduates, ranging in age from 25 to 39 years old, who attended two- and four-year institutions were asked the following survey questions.

Percentage

Do you think the college you attended charged a fair price?

79% Yes

53% Yes

Do you think the price of higher education is too high?

65% Yes

Public College Graduates

Private College Graduates

Graduates from Private and Public Colleges

Taken from: *Inside Higher Ed*, "Alumni Perceptions of Price and Other Matters," May 20, 2008.

Making a Candid Case Has Worked for Reed College

Making a candid case regarding college costs is an approach I have seen work for Reed College. In information sessions, when I have justified Reed's tuition charges using images of artisans and craftsmen to describe what goes into a Reed education, I have seen the description resonate with audiences. I believe that those audiences have responded positively because they understand that they usually pay more for individually tailored and handcrafted items that have an inherent quality advantage built into them. Just as most people recognize the value of seeing or being part of a live, rather than a recorded, performance or of getting a poem or artwork created specifically for them, rather than receiving a mass-produced card, they understand the value of a handcrafted education.

The students and parents I speak to seem to appreciate that Reed addresses the high cost issue directly and offers an explanation that sounds consistent with the values and the day-to-day academic life of the college. They also seem to understand that a small college like Reed provides a highly personalized education—where every student has the apprentice scholar experience of a thesis—that cannot easily be replicated at a lower cost. The idea that life changing goes on in addition to degree acquisition is a powerful closer—to use sales parlance—for Reed.

In the midst of brick throwing at colleges over rising costs, Reed has chosen to make its here-is-why-we-cost-so-much case by citing the value of its handcrafted education. The approach works for Reed because it reflects the college's mission and communicates institutional values. But the approach also works because Reed has constructed a narrative about college costs that makes sense and sounds believable rather than like defensive back pedaling or dissembling. Perhaps by tying their explanations of rising college costs to their distinctive missions and identities other colleges and universities can craft similar persuasive narratives.

EVALUATING THE AUTHORS' ARGUMENTS:

In this viewpoint, Paul Marthers says it is wrong to treat a college education like a commodity and colleges like businesses. In the previous viewpoint, Richard Vedder says college costs could be reduced if colleges were run more like businesses. Who do you think is right and why? Support your opinion with examples from the viewpoints.

Merit-Based Financial Aid Limits Access to College

Mark Clayton

"[Harvard University's Civil Rights Project's new analysis] warns of negative consequences to American society if such [merit scholarship] programs 'lead to larger wage and income gaps along racial lines.'"

In the following viewpoint, Mark Clayton discusses Harvard University's Civil Right Project, an analysis titled, "Merit Scholarships: Who Is Really Being Served?" Clayton says that Harvard's analysis is a warning of what might happen to American society at large if merit-based scholarship programs continue to take affect. This is because under a merit-based financial aid system, academic merit is the basis for granting aid, not a student's economic situation. Based on the report, Clayton contends that merit-based programs are shifting the public educational funding away from the neediest and toward more funding for affluent students, students that would have gone to college regardless of a scholarship. Mark Clayton is a staff writer for the *Christian Science Monitor*.

Mark Clayton, "Merit Scholarships: Robin Hood in Reverse?" *The Christian Science Monitor*, August 27, 2002. Reproduced by permission from *The Christian Science Monitor* (www.csmonitor.com).

1. What is Georgia's HOPE program? Based on Harvard's analysis, how might programs like these affect American society at large?
2. Why is access such a critical issue?
3. According to Antonio Flores of the Hispanic Association of Colleges and Universities, how are merit-based scholarships like "Robin Hood in reverse"?

G eorgia's highly touted HOPE scholarship program, which doles out state college-tuition dollars to high school seniors who graduate with at least a B average, has been hugely popular since it began in 1993. Nearly a dozen states followed its lead and started their own "merit-based" scholarships funded by taxpayers. The federal government has its own version too.

But a new analysis, "Merit Scholarships: Who Is Really Being Served?" released yesterday by Harvard University's Civil Rights Project, points to a host of problems in the four states studied. It warns of negative consequences to American society if such programs "lead to larger wage and income gaps along racial lines."

FAST FACT

In 2006–2007, about 75 percent of full-time undergraduate college students received some form of financial aid, according to the College Board.

The Importance of Access to College

The laudable goals of such scholarship plans have been to promote college access to those who might not attend, encourage hard-working students, and slow the "brain drain" by giving the best students incentive to attend college in their home state.

Access is a critical issue because states are wrestling with how to open the doors of college to minorities and low-income students even as higher-education budgets are being slashed. And higher education is more critical than ever to finding a well-paying job. But the unintended consequences of these programs, the report says, include:

- In Florida and Michigan, the highest proportion of merit scholarships were awarded to students graduating from high schools that already had the highest college-participation rates.
- In New Mexico, 80 percent of scholarship recipients were from families earning more than $40,000 per year, well above the state's median income of about $32,000.
- Georgia, which has the nation's largest such program, spent $300 million on HOPE (Helping Outstanding Pupils Educationally) in 2000–01. But only 4 percent of the funds resulted in increased college access in the state, while 96 percent of scholarships went to students who would have attended college anyway.

Less Money for Those Who Need It Most

The latter result seems to be part of a broader shift away from public funding for the neediest and toward more funding for affluent students. Among the nation's 12 state merit-aid programs, $863 million in scholarships was handed out during the 2000–01 academic year, about triple the $308 million states provided in need-based aid.

"What this report shows is that public money is not being spent on those who need it—but on those who don't," says Antonio Flores, president of the Hispanic Association of Colleges and Universities,

Many low- or middle-income students, despite good SAT scores, are unfairly turned down for financial aid.

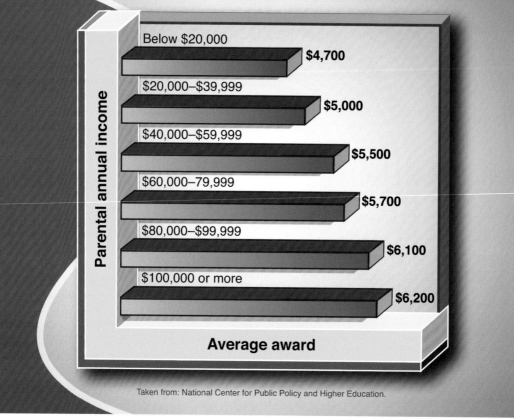

Unfair Aid?

Middle- and upper-income undergraduates receive larger grants from schools than do low-income students.

Parental annual income

Below $20,000 — **$4,700**

$20,000–$39,999 — **$5,000**

$40,000–$59,999 — **$5,500**

$60,000–79,999 — **$5,700**

$80,000–$99,999 — **$6,100**

$100,000 or more — **$6,200**

Average award

Taken from: National Center for Public Policy and Higher Education.

a lobby group based in San Antonio, Texas. "It's almost like Robin Hood in reverse."

This is one of the key findings of the in-depth look at merit-scholarship programs in Georgia, Michigan, New Mexico, and Florida. "Many students who were already headed to college get funds even though they may not need them," writes coauthor Patricia Marin, a Harvard professor. "In the meantime, students who need financial support to attend college have seen slower growth in need-based aid," she continues.

The study is the first comprehensive analysis of such programs based on data rather than anecdotes, says coauthor Donald Heller, an associate professor and senior research associate at Pennsylvania State University's Center for the Study of Higher Education.

"We're not saying there shouldn't be merit scholarships," he says. "But do we really want Ted Turner's kid to get this scholarship? Maybe people who read this report will ask themselves, 'Do we really want to give these scholarships to kids from families making $100,000 to $500,000 a year?'" Such comments and findings are anathema in Georgia—and perhaps in the 11 other states with similar programs that have quickly become beloved by middle- and upper-middle-class voters.

Merit Scholarships Makes Room for "Extras"

Richard McCook and his daughter Brandy are some of the devotees of Georgia's HOPE scholarship. Attending college was never a question for Brandy McCook. An honors student at her suburban high school near Atlanta, she was going no matter what. Even so, she got about $30,000 in state merit-scholarship funds to attend the University of Georgia the past four years, her father estimates.

Those tuition payments have been terrific, says Mr. McCook, who owns a driving school in the Atlanta area. His other daughter, too, got the same HOPE scholarship. All that public funding for his kids' college left him with cash to pay for some nice extras. "Having that scholarship money meant we were able to do more for them," Mr. McCook says. "Both girls are in a sorority—and we gave both of them cars. Brandy got a Chevrolet Cavalier and we got her older sister, April, a Mazda Miata."

EVALUATING THE AUTHOR'S ARGUMENTS:

Mark Clayton is a reporter for the *Christian Science Monitor*. It is his job as a reporter to present both sides of an issue objectively, fairly, and accurately. Clayton used many of his sources' quotes throughout his piece. Do you think Clayton did his job and reported each side equally? If not, what do you think Clayton's opinion on the issue of merit-based financial aid is? Explain your answer.

Merit-Based Financial Aid Does Not Limit Access to College

Daniel F. Sullivan

"Merit aid, which the majority of our wealthy competitors do not provide, is key to our ability to enroll more low-income students."

In the following viewpoint Daniel F. Sullivan contends that ending merit-based aid, as many elite colleges are doing, will not increase the numbers of low-income students at America's colleges and universities. Merit-based aid does not limit college access, says Sullivan. In fact, Sullivan asserts that providing merit-based aid actually helps his college, St. Lawrence, enroll more low-income students. Sullivan points a finger at wealthy colleges and says they hold the key to increasing the socioeconomic diversity of America's colleges and universities. Sullivan is president of St. Lawrence University in Canton, New York.

AS YOU READ, CONSIDER THE FOLLOWING QUESTIONS:

1. According to Sullivan, what proportion of St. Lawrence University students are recipients of federal Pell Grants? What proportion of Williams College students received Pell Grants in 2003–2004?

Daniel F. Sullivan, "Merit and Access," *Inside Higher Ed,* April 19, 2007. Reproduced by permission.

2. What does a study by Catherine Hill and Gordon Winston show, as stated by Sullivan?
3. According to the author, what are two other public goods that would result from changed behavior at elite colleges and universities?

The crisis of access to higher education by students from low- and moderate-income families is likely to be made worse, not better, if other colleges and universities follow the lead of a small number of very wealthy private colleges and universities to eliminate merit aid and provide aid packages for their students that do not include student loans.

Ending Merit Aid Will Not Solve National Crisis

These well-publicized moves will not provide full access. Ending merit aid and student loans at a small number of institutions will not change the fact that nationally, high-achieving students from low-income families still have no more chance of graduating from college than do low-achievers from high-income families. That is the real crisis, and it is a national disgrace. As a nation, we are failing to get anywhere near enough of the best students from low-income families motivated and able to afford to attend college.

In recent weeks we have seen a number of commentaries and announcements from colleges and universities meant to show how they are addressing this issue. Some institutions have announced that they will no longer award merit aid to students. These announcements have been met with almost universal acclaim. Advocates argue that merit aid will no longer be "wasted" on students who do not need it to attend college. They say that money now can somehow be reallocated to needy students, and institutions that continue to provide merit aid are doing so merely and shamefully to increase the number of students with high test scores so that they can achieve a higher *U.S. News & World Report* ranking. If funds formerly used for merit aid are reallocated to an institution's existing needy students, that is great for them, but unless such institutions do something to increase the number of able low-income students in their applicant pools, this will not solve our crisis.

Several other private institutions have announced that they will no longer require students who receive financial aid to take out loans to help finance their education—their entire financial need will be met with grants. . . .

Wealthy Colleges Not Enrolling Enough Low-Income Students

Let me tell you what is really going on with these moves by wealthy private colleges and universities to drop merit aid and eliminate student loan debt.

The answers may be found most readily in an outstanding recent book: *Equity and Excellence in American Higher Education*, by William G. Bowen, Martin A. Kurzweil and Eugene M. Tobin. Here are the key facts. The wealthiest colleges and universities—those that can best afford the financial aid necessary to enroll large numbers of low-income students—in fact enroll the smallest percentages of

College financial aid counselors are struggling to admit low-income students because the government has stopped funding some financial-aid education programs.

such students. In their attempt to seek or maintain the highest possible competitive position with regard to academic reputation, these institutions seek to maximize the average test scores of their incoming students. Test scores are highly correlated with family income—the higher the family income, the higher the test scores. Because only students with high test scores apply to these institutions, low-income students are underrepresented in their applicant pools.

After making exceptions for legacies (the children of alumni families), some minority groups and recruited athletes, these institutions then admit students on a need-blind basis. These institutions have the resources to meet the full financial need of admitted students, which means admitted low-income students can afford to enroll, and they will make up roughly the same percentage of enrolled students as they are in the qualified applicant pool. The public and the media applaud these institutions for their commitment to low-income students because they have admitted them on a need-blind basis and met their full need. There is the suggestion that if only institutions like St. Lawrence would follow their lead, all would be well in America on the question of access to college for low-income students—NOT!

Colleges cannot admit those who do not apply in the first place. Since family income is correlated with academic preparation, I submit that colleges will not improve access in any demonstrable way unless they give low-income students already in their applicant pools an admissions preference and/or they take major steps to increase the percentage of low-income students in their applicant pools. This isn't just about financial aid, but about which students colleges admit.

Merit Aid *and* More Low-Income Students

A selective undergraduate liberal arts college that is moderately well-off financially, St. Lawrence has an endowment of about $250 million for 2,150 students and raises about $20 million in gifts from private sources annually. We provide merit aid to about a third of our students and graduate students with a relatively high average debt load. Twenty percent of our students are recipients of federal Pell Grants, the grants that go to students from the lowest-quartile of family incomes in America. For the elite, highly endowed institutions that were studied for *Equity and Excellence,* the average percentage of enrolled students from this quartile was 10.8 percent. Williams, with an endowment of almost $1.5 billion in 2006, had 10.6 percent of its students receiving Pell Grants in 2003–04; Middlebury: $800 million endowment, 9.4 percent Pell recipients; Pomona $1.5 billion endowment, 10.2 percent Pell recipients; Swarthmore: $1.4 billion endowment, 12.3 percent Pell recipients.

Seventy-five percent of St. Lawrence students received institutionally funded scholarships, while 41 percent of Williams' students do, 36 percent for Middlebury, 57 percent for Pomona, and 53 percent for Swarthmore. St. Lawrence's institutionally funded student grant aid budget is, on an enrollment-adjusted basis, $7.5 million higher than Williams', $5.4 million higher than Middlebury's, $3.9 million higher than Pomona's, and $4.8 million higher than Swarthmore's. St. Lawrence students who have received financial aid graduate with more debt than students from these colleges, but they graduate at the same high rate as students who do not receive financial aid. Which institutions are making a larger contribution to the education of low-income students? I guess the answer depends on one's perspective. The low-income students enrolled at our wealthiest private colleges and universities receive a truly marvelous education and graduate with less debt, but there are far fewer of them at those institutions than at institutions like mine.

More Low-Income Students *Because* of Merit Aid

Merit aid, which the majority of our wealthy competitors do not provide, is key to our ability to enroll more low-income students. Here's how it works:

- The merit aid our students with need receive is a partial substitute for need-based aid for which they would otherwise be eligible. We are very clear in our published financial aid information about this.
- Students receiving merit aid have a higher percentage of their need met by grants rather than loans, so they carry a lower debt load at graduation.
- For students qualifying for merit aid who do not have financial need or whose merit aid exceeds need, merit aid lowers the cost of attendance directly.

- In both cases, providing merit aid increases the probability that such students will enroll at St. Lawrence.
- Without providing merit aid to some students who have no financial need, fewer of them would enroll.
- There is indeed a positive impact on our student profile from their enrollment, but the average merit-aided no-need student pays St. Lawrence more in net tuition than the average St. Lawrence student pays. This is how we are able to afford to enroll so many more low-income students.

We believe that one of our responsibilities as a leading liberal arts college is to do our share of the educating of low-income students. This is a noble motive, not a base motive, and even though we do provide merit aid, the resulting distribution of student and family cost of attendance by family income is highly progressive. . . .

Wealthy Colleges Still Enroll Few Low-Income Students

I have pressed this logic on presidential colleagues from wealthier institutions without much success. They continue to believe that the only approach to student aid that captures the moral high ground is the approach their institutions use, which does not alter the reality that they enroll very few low-income students, as Bowen et al. have shown. Until this writing I have avoided talking in public about these matters in this way, outside of my own institution, so as not to appear merely defensive. However, the unwillingness of presidents like me to speak out is resulting in a serious misunderstanding by the public and by federal and state legislators of the national student aid and family cost of education picture. This then leads to an inability to define and fund appropriate public policies.

My presidential colleagues from wealthier institutions do not have to provide merit aid because their academic reputations and wealth allows them to attract high ability students from high-income families

> **FAST FACT**
>
> Most federal Pell Grants awarded in the 2005–2006 academic year (about 39 percent) were awarded to students attending two-year community colleges.

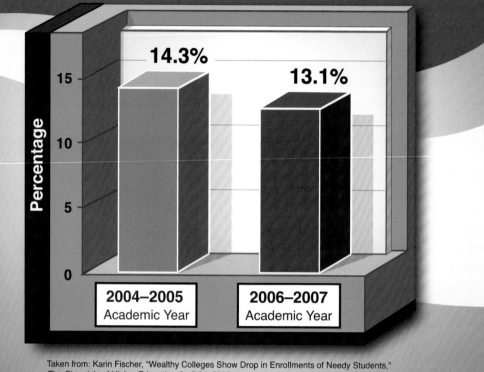

Wealthy Colleges Show a Drop in Enrollment of Needy Students

Percent of Pell Grant Recipients at the 75 Wealthiest American Colleges

Taken from: Karin Fischer, "Wealthy Colleges Show Drop in Enrollments of Needy Students," *The Chronicle of Higher Education*, April 24, 2008.

without it. That means, actually, that they have even more flexibility to enroll low-income students than we do at St. Lawrence. Why don't they use their financial flexibility for this noble purpose? I hope the recent decisions of some institutions on merit aid and student loans do result in their enrolling more low-income students. . . .

Enough Low-Income Students with Ability

Some have suggested that, even if elite institutions were to seek to enroll more low-income students, not enough of them are out there who have the ability and preparation to benefit. But a study by Catherine B. Hill and Gordon C. Winston shows clearly that there are indeed more than enough low-income, high-ability students who could thrive in the academic environments of the most selective colleges to allow them to have student bodies that would mirror the overall distribution of American families socio-economically. This would mean, however, that these institutions would have to increase their financial aid budgets (they can afford it) and decrease their commitment to maximizing the average SAT scores of their incoming class, and for many of these institutions that is unthinkable. While some of these elite colleges say that they do this now, the incredibly small numbers of low-income students most enroll suggests that they don't do so nearly enough.

Colleagues from such institutions respond . . . that . . . all it would do is move low-income students from institutions like St. Lawrence to their wealthier competitors, with no net increase in the number of low-income students attending college. I believe they are wrong. In the 1980s, college enrollments grew steadily, despite a 35 percent decline in the number of high school graduates. That was made possible because colleges and universities, scrambling to maintain enrollment, re-tooled themselves to help able students with less adequate high school preparations succeed, and many institutions also broadened their markets by enrolling older and international students. With institutional commitment and appropriate public policy, I firmly believe we could again expand the pool of able low-income students enrolled in our colleges.

Wealthy Colleges Could Increase Socio-Economic Diversity

There are two other public goods that would result from changed behavior among the elite and wealthy private colleges and universities. More low-income students would benefit from the wonderful richness and quality these highly selective institutions provide if more were enrolled. And very importantly, these institutions—very influential opinion leaders in American higher education—could do the same for socio-economic diversity as they did for racial diversity several decades ago. By committing to be racially and ethnically diverse, for reasons of social justice and because of the educational value of such diversity, after a history of exclusion, these institutions helped set the bar for the rest of us. They are now very diverse ethnically and racially, and they set the standard that I aspire to at St. Lawrence. I believe they should do the same with regard to socio-economic diversity. If they do, we will make more progress faster in the nation as a whole.

Instead, we are hearing arguments for the elimination of merit aid at institutions like St. Lawrence, and that students and their families should not have to treat a college education like a long-term investment financed, like a house, by some debt. This reasoning deflects attention away from the poor job I believe our most wealthy private institutions are doing with regard to socio-economic diversity. If recruited athletes can have a 35 percent admissions advantage and legacies a 20 percent admissions advantage, surely students from low-income families can also have an admissions advantage. Providing merit aid and expecting needy students to finance part of their education with debt helps St. Lawrence afford to have the high level of socio-economic diversity that we do. Our path to achieving that diversity, a product of our particular history and circumstances, may be different from the path a wealthier institution might take, but it is still a noble path, given the ends and the outcomes.

EVALUATING THE AUTHOR'S ARGUMENTS:

In this viewpoint Daniel F. Sullivan contends that merit-based financial aid does not limit college access to low-income students, while in the previous viewpoint, Mark Clayton contends that it does. What specific points do the authors disagree upon? What specific points do they agree upon? Which viewpoint do you think was more persuasive and why?

Viewpoint

5

Standardized Tests Should Be Eliminated in College Admissions

Nathan O. Hatch

"This step away from standardized tests will help us and other institutions of higher education move closer to the goals of greater educational quality and opportunity."

In the following viewpoint Nathan O. Hatch explains why his college, Wake Forest, is eliminating the use of standardized test scores as a requirement for college admission. According to Hatch, the SAT college admission test is one of the major reasons that there is such a wide disparity between high- and low-income students' college enrollment rates. Hatch says that by moving away from standardized testing, Wake Forest and other colleges can achieve greater diversity and increase educational opportunities for people from all socioeconomic backgrounds. Hatch became the president of Wake Forest University in 2005. Before that he was a history professor and provost at Notre Dame University.

Nathan O. Hatch, "R.I.P. SAT?" *The Record,* July 2, 2008, p. A13. Copyright © 2008 North Jersey Media Group, Inc. Reproduced by permission by the author.

AS YOU READ, CONSIDER THE FOLLOWING QUESTIONS:
1. According to Hatch, in 1970 what percent of students from the lowest-income families earned a bachelor's degree by the age of twenty-four? According to Hatch, has this number changed?
2. According to Hatch, what two factors are better predictors of college performance than the SAT?
3. According to Hatch, starting with the coming year's admission cycle (2009) what will Wake Forest be adding to the admission process to replace the SAT?

The College Board amended its policy on reporting SAT scores this month in an effort to ease stress on student test takers. While all scores are currently reported to colleges students apply to, starting with the Class of 2010 students who take the entrance examination multiple times will be able to control which of their scores admissions officers see. Even before then, though, students who want to attend Wake Forest University won't have to worry quite so much about the exam that most universities rely on so heavily.

FAST FACT

Eleven percent of the 1.5 million SAT takers in the 2008 high school graduating class were black, according to the College Board.

Last month, Wake Forest dropped the SAT and ACT as an entrance requirement, becoming the only top-30 national university with a test-optional policy. This step away from standardized tests will help us and other institutions of higher education move closer to the goals of greater educational quality and opportunity.

Our decision to reevaluate our admissions policy grew out of a close look at the state of higher education and some long, hard thinking about the kind of university we want Wake Forest to be. For several years, a growing body of research has made clear that America's top colleges and universities are doing a poor job of helping some young people realize a critical part of the American dream: that anyone, no matter where he or she begins in life, has the chance to rise to the top.

Disparity in Acceptance Rates

For example, students from the top quarter of the socioeconomic hierarchy are 25 times more likely to attend a "top-tier" college than students from the bottom quarter. In 1970, only 6 percent of students from the lowest-income families earned a bachelor's degree by age 24. More than 30 years later, the figure was still only 6 percent.

Research has indicated that one of the major reasons equal opportunity is lacking is universities' reliance on standardized tests, such as the SAT. Analyses show clearly that performance on the SAT is

According to the author of this viewpoint, the SAT college admissions test is one of the major reasons there is a disparity between high- and low-income students who attend college.

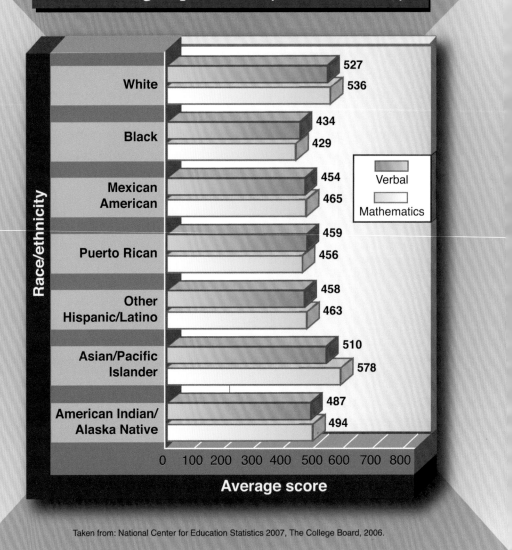

Average SAT Scores for 12th-Grade SAT Test-Taking Population, by Race/Ethnicity

Race/ethnicity	Verbal	Mathematics
White	527	536
Black	434	429
Mexican American	454	465
Puerto Rican	459	456
Other Hispanic/Latino	458	463
Asian/Pacific Islander	510	578
American Indian/Alaska Native	487	494

Taken from: National Center for Education Statistics 2007, The College Board, 2006.

closely correlated with family income. Two scholars recently found that top colleges and universities could increase the enrollment of low-income students simply by giving greater weight to admissions criteria other than standardized tests.

Some argue that this limited opportunity is the price universities have to pay for a quality student body. But the research and our experience don't bear this out. A study of 78,000 students in California found that SAT scores correlated with family income but not with college grades.

In fact, the SAT was the poorest predictor of college performance when compared with high school grades and performance on subject tests.

Other studies have found that such factors as high school class ranking and strength of the high school course load are better predictors. A 2007 analysis of national data sets, for example, showed that colleges can attain both academic excellence and social diversity if they base admissions on high school grade-point average and class rank, but not if they depend on SAT scores.

For all of these reasons, some of the nation's top small liberal arts colleges like Bates, Hamilton, Holy Cross, Middlebury and Bowdoin have moved away from the SAT and achieved greater diversity and quality in their student bodies. By making the SAT optional at Wake Forest University, we hope to encourage the momentum for change among the nation's most selective institutions.

The Wrong Message

Above all, however, we want to ensure that Wake Forest is true to its ideals and mission. We are well prepared, because this is a place that prizes its commitment to opportunity. We have always reviewed every application to Wake Forest, read and evaluated the essays, and weighed a range of factors. But we thought that our SAT requirement sent students the opposite message that in the end what counted was performance on a standardized test.

So, starting with the coming year's [2009] admission cycle, a standardized test score will no longer be mandatory for admission here. Instead, we will be adding more personalized elements, including a recommended personal interview and additional opportunities to demonstrate individuality. Students can send us their SAT scores if they want them to be considered in the evaluation process, but they will not be required.

This step aligns our admission policies with our mission as a university. By opening doors even wider to qualified students from all backgrounds and circumstances, we believe we are sending a powerful message of inclusion and advocating for democracy of access to higher education.

We also hope it will advance the emerging national discussion of equal opportunity, quality and the SAT, and perhaps renew higher education's role in achieving the American dream.

EVALUATING THE AUTHOR'S ARGUMENTS:

Nathan O. Hatch contends that colleges should abandon the use of the SAT as a college admission requirement in order to provide greater access to college for low-income families. What evidence does he use to support his contention that the SAT is harmful for diversity?

Standardized Tests Should Not Be Eliminated in College Admissions

"For better or worse, the SAT is probably not going anywhere, anytime soon."

Tim Goral

In the following viewpoint, Tim Goral maintains that the SAT will continue to be used for college admissions. Despite its critics, the test has been improved and the results now have more meaning, Goral argues. The new writing section of the test has caused high schools to focus more on the subject, which has resulted in more prepared college students. Several studies have also shown that the writing portion of the test can accurately predict first-year college grades. Tim Goral is the editor in chief of *University Business* magazine.

AS YOU READ, CONSIDER THE FOLLOWING QUESTIONS:

1. What does Goral have to say about why the SAT will still be used in college admissions?

Tim Goral, "The SAT Is Dead; Long Live the SAT," *University Business*, vol. 11, August 2008, p. 10. Copyright © 2008 Professional Media Group LLC. Reproduced by permission.

2. What does the author think about William Zinsser and his books on writing?
3. What studies does Goral use to support his point about the SAT writing section predicting first-year college grades?

Every month, it seems, we hear of another institution deciding to make the SAT an optional part of the admissions process. Other schools combine SAT scores with a student's high school records to get a more rounded picture. Still other colleges have decided to eliminate the test altogether.

The SAT, which was introduced in 1901, has become so entrenched as part of the process of going to college that a multibillion dollar industry has grown up around it. Test preparation books, high-priced coaches, weekend workshops, practice tests, and more all claim to give students an advantage when they take the test.

FAST FACT

The number of SAT takers in the 2008 high school graduating class rose to 1,518,859, an 8 percent increase from 2003, and a 29.5 percent increase from 1998, according to the College Board.

That's part of the argument of those who would prefer to see the SAT go away—high scores show little more than that the student had prepared well for the test.

But how do you get rid of it? No one seems to know. If, for example, a decision was made that no school would use the test after 2015, would the classes of 2013 and 2014 decide to wait until after the deadline passes to apply to college? What impact would that have on tuition dependent institutions? For better or worse, the SAT is probably not going anywhere, anytime soon.

But that's no reason the SAT can't be improved so that its results have real meaning. And it has.

The Importance of Writing

Some years ago I became a fan of William Zinsser, whose books on writing inspired me and countless others. In his book *Writing to*

Learn, Zinsser described the concept of writing across the curriculum, then being tested at Gustavus Adolphus College (Minn.). The idea is that writing should be an integral part of every discipline, whether it is history, science, or even physical education. It's one thing, Zinsser said, for a math student to be able to solve an equation, but it is quite another for that student to be able to convey in writing how the answer was reached so that another person, unfamiliar with the subject, might learn as well. Such an approach would demonstrate not only learning but also understanding.

The author of this viewpoint thinks that Wake Forest University's policy of making the SAT test optional will degrade the institution's academic reputation.

The Number of High School Graduates Who Take the SAT Varies Significantly

Percentage of high school students who took the SAT in 2005–2006. The national average was 48 percent.

WA 54%		
OR 55%	MT 28%	ND 4%
ID 19%	MN 10%	NH 82%
	VT 67%	ME 73%

NH 82%
VT 67%
ME 73%

WA 54%
MT 28%
ND 4%
MN 10%
WI 6%
MI 10%
NY 88%
MA 85%

OR 55%
ID 19%
SD 4%
PA 74%
RI 69%
CT 84%

WY 10%
NE 7%
IA 4%
IL 9%
IN 62%
OH 28%
WV 20%
VA 73%
NJ 82%
DE 73%

NV 40%
UT 7%
CO 26%
KS 8%
MO 7%
KY 11%
NC 71%
MD 70%
D.C. 78%

CA 49%
AZ 32%
NM 13%
OK 7%
AR 5%
TN 15%
SC 62%

MS 4%
AL 9%
GA 70%

TX 52%
LA 6%
FL 65%

AK 51%

HI 60%

Taken from: National Center for Education Statistics, 2006.

At the time, as an idealistic college graduate, I tried to introduce Zinsser's book to my local board of education. Sadly, their agenda, then as now, was more devoted to budget questions than possible tweaks to the curriculum. So three years ago [2005], when The College Board introduced SAT II, with its increased emphasis on writing, I had high hopes. Would these new tests be a more accurate reflection of learning?

Last month [July 2008], The College Board released new "SAT Validity Studies" that support the argument that the expanded writing section of the test is more predictive of a student's first-year grades in college than the math or critical reading sections. These conclusions are also supported elsewhere.

According to an article in the *Christian Science Monitor*, an independent study by researchers at The University of Georgia Terry College of Business shows the SAT writing section predicts more than just first-year college grades. According to the study, for every 100 points more students scored on the 800-point writing test, first-year students gained .07 on a 4-point GPA scale.

"Since the SAT added writing, high schools in this nation are focusing more on teaching writing," said Laurence Bunin, senior vice president for the SAT, in the article. "That's really important for students—for their readiness for college and success in college."

I can't agree more.

EVALUATING THE AUTHORS' ARGUMENTS:

In this viewpoint, Tim Goral argues that colleges should continue to use the SAT as part of their admissions process. In the previous viewpoint, Nathan Hatch maintains that colleges should drop SAT scores as a college admission requirement. Which viewpoint do you agree with and why? Use examples from the viewpoints to support your opinion.

Editor's note: These facts can be used in reports or papers to reinforce or add credibility when making important points or claims.

Supply and Demand
According to the National Center for Education Statistics:

- In the 2007–2008 academic year, 6,551 postsecondary institutions were in the United States. Among these,
  - 2,004 were public institutions,
  - 2,732 were private for-profit institutions, and
  - 1,815 were private nonprofit institutions.

- During 2007–2008, the average cost of attendance at four-year postsecondary institutions for full-time undergraduates living on campus were:
  - $33,029 for private for-profit institutions,
  - $31,019 for private nonprofit institutions,
  - $16,758 for public institutions (in-state students), and
  - $24,955 for public institutions (out-of-state students).

- During the 2006–2007 academic year, 14,853,710 full-time students were enrolled in postsecondary institutions. Among these,
  - 6,010,715 were enrolled at public four-year institutions,
  - 4,068,495 were enrolled at public two-year institutions,
  - 2,988,238 were enrolled at private nonprofit four-year institutions, and
  - 919,164 were enrolled at private for-profit four-year institutions.

College Degrees Awarded
According to the National Center for Education Statistics:

- During the 2006–2007 academic year, four-year institutions awarded about 2.4 million degrees. Among these,
  - 42 percent were awarded to men, and
  - 58 percent were awarded to women.

- During the 2006–2007 academic year, two-year institutions awarded about 564,000 degrees. Among these,
  - 37 percent were awarded to men, and
  - 63 percent were awarded to women.
- During the 2006–2007 academic year, 1,524,092 bachelor degrees were awarded. Among these,
  - 449,830 were awarded to white men,
  - 582,932 were awarded to white women,
  - 46,425 were awarded to black men,
  - 90,996 were awarded to black women,
  - 41,819 were awarded to Hispanic men, and
  - 65,897 were awarded to Hispanic women.
- In the 2005–2006 academic year, 1,485,242 bachelor degrees were granted. Among these,
  - 21 percent were in business,
  - 11 percent were in social sciences and history,
  - 7 percent were in education,
  - 6 percent were in health professions,
  - 6 percent were in psychology,
  - 5 percent were in communications and journalism,
  - 4.7 percent were in biological sciences,
  - 4.5 percent were in engineering,
  - 1.6 percent were in agriculture and natural resources, and
  - 1 percent were in mathematics and statistics.

College Students

According the Higher Education Research Institute's *2008 Your First College Year (YFCY) Survey:*

- Nearly three-fourths of first-year college students surveyed reported being "satisfied" or "very satisfied" with their overall college experience.

- Close to one-third of the survey respondents felt intimidated by their professors in the first college year.

- The majority of respondents felt "completely successful" in developing close friendships with other students.

- The majority of first-year students have some degree of concern about financing their college education, although less than one-third of the respondents work for pay on or off campus.

- Less than half of the students "frequently" felt overwhelmed, lonely, or homesick and worried about meeting new people in the first year.

- Students reported mostly positive interactions with their peers since entering college.

- Slightly more than one-third of the respondents interacted with family members on a daily basis.

- As compared with when they entered college, first-year students
  - spend more time studying, partying, and socializing with friends;
  - spend less time attending to household or childcare duties, exercising, performing volunteer work, attending religious services, and reading for pleasure;
  - drink beer, wine, and/or other types of liquor more frequently;
  - feel more overwhelmed and depressed; and
  - feel less worried about the costs of college.

College Diversity

According to the American Council on Education:

- Total minority enrollment at the nation's colleges and universities rose by 50 percent from 3.4 million students to 5 million students between 1995 and 2005.

- White enrollment increased from 9.9 million to 10.7 million, a gain of 8 percent between 1995 and 2005.

- In 2006, 61 percent of Asian Americans aged 18 to 24 were enrolled in college compared with 44 percent of whites, 32 percent of African Americans, and 25 percent of Hispanics and Native Americans respectively.

- College enrollment among African Americans rose by 46 percent between 1995 and 2005 to nearly 2 million students.

- The increase in Hispanic enrollment between 1995 and 2005 led all racial/ethnic groups, up by 66 percent to more than 1.7 million students. Hispanic enrollment grew faster at four-year institutions than at two-year institutions.

- Asian-American enrollment increased to more than 1 million over the ten-year period between 1995 and 2005, up 37 percent.

- Native American enrollment grew by 31 percent in the ten-year period, up from nearly 127,000 in 1995 to nearly 167,000 in 2005.

- Thirty-six percent of young men aged 19 to 24 were enrolled in college in 2006 compared with 44 percent of young women.

- Among students who began at two-year institutions in 2003, 55 percent were still enrolled or had attained a certificate or degree anywhere in higher education three years later.

- Among students who began at a four-year institution in 2003, 81 percent were still enrolled or had attained a certificate or degree anywhere in higher education three years later.

Community College

According to the National Center for Education Statistics:

- In 2006–2007 1,045 community colleges were in the United States, enrolling 6.2 million students (or 35 percent of all post-secondary students enrolled that year).

- Average annual community college tuition and fees are less than half those at public four-year colleges and universities and one-tenth those at private four-year colleges and universities.

- Community colleges have larger percentages of nontraditional, low-income, and minority students than four-year colleges and universities.

- High school seniors who enrolled immediately in community colleges in 2004 spanned a broad range of academic achievement— including students who were well prepared for college in terms of their performance on standardized tests and coursework completed.

- In 2004, 28 percent of high school seniors who enrolled immediately in a community college planned to use it as a stepping-stone to a bachelor's degree.

- In 2004 one-third of seniors who enrolled immediately in a community college did so with no intention of pursuing any education higher than an associate's degree; however, by 2006 almost 47 percent of this group had raised their educational expectations to start or complete a bachelor's degree.

Organizations to Contact

The editors have compiled the following list of organizations concerned with the issues debated in this book. The descriptions are derived from materials provided by the organizations. All have publications or information available for interested readers. The list was compiled on the date of publication of the present volume; the information provided here may change. Be aware that many organizations take several weeks or longer to respond to queries, so allow as much time as possible.

American Council on Education (ACE)
One Dupont Circle NW
Washington, DC 20036-1193
(202) 939-9300
e-mail: comments@ace.nche.edu
Web site: www.acenet.edu

The American Council on Education (ACE) is a higher education organization representing presidents and chancellors of all types of U.S. accredited, degree-granting institutions. ACE represents the interests of college executives; speaks as higher education's voice in matters of public policy; provides vital programs, information, and a forum for dialogue on key issues. The council issues the biweekly e-mail newsletter *Higher Education and National Affairs* as well as several periodic papers and special reports.

Council for Opportunity in Education
1025 Vermont Ave. NW, Ste. 900
Washington, DC 2005
(202) 347-7430
Web site: www.coenet.us

The Council for Opportunity in Education is a nonprofit organization dedicated to furthering the expansion of educational opportunities for low-income, first generation, and minority students throughout the

United States. The council works in conjunction with colleges, universities, and agencies that host TRIO Programs. TRIO Programs are a series of programs, such as Upward Bound and Talent Search, funded under Title IV of the Higher Education Act of 1965 to help Americans overcome class, social, and cultural barriers to higher education.

Editorial Projects in Education Inc. (EPE)
6935 Arlington Rd., Ste. 100
Bethesda, MD 20814-5233
e-mail: webeditors@epe.org
Web site: www.edweek.org

Editorial Projects in Education Inc. is a nonprofit organization whose primary mission is to help raise the level of public awareness and understanding of important issues in American education from preschool through the twelfth grade. EPE publishes several journals, including *Education Week,* the *Teacher Professional Development Sourcebook,* and *Digital Directions.*

The Education Trust
1250 H St. NW, Ste. 700
Washington, DC 20005
(202) 293-1217
e-mail: www2.edtrust.org
Web site: www2.edtrust.org

The Education Trust is funded by several philanthropic foundations. The trust's mission is to facilitate the high academic achievement of all students at all levels and close the achievement gaps that separate low-income students and students of color from other youth. The organization offers several online tools, which students and parents can use to examine achievement and opportunity patterns at schools by race, ethnicity, and family income. The Education Trust publishes a range of publications about the achievement gap and what can be done to close it.

Educational Policy Institute (EPI)
2401 Seaboard Rd., Ste. 104
Virginia Beach, VA 23456
(757) 430-2200
e-mail: wswail@educationalpolicy.org
Web site: www.educationalpolicy.org

The Educational Policy Institute is a nonprofit organization dedicated to the study of issues related to the expansion of quality educational opportunities. The organization seeks to expand educational opportunity for low-income and other historically underrepresented students through high-level research and analysis. EPI publishes several newsletters, including *EPICenter, Commentary,* and *Student Success.*

Educational Testing Services (ETS)
Rosedale Rd.
Princeton, NJ 08541
(609) 921-9000
Web site: www.ets.org

Educational Testing Services (ETS) is a nonprofit organization that develops and administers many standardized educational programs and tests, such as the Advanced Placement (AP) program and the SAT test. ETS publishes the magazine *Innovations,* which provides information on educational assessment for educators, school leaders, researchers, and policy makers around the world.

Higher Education Research Institute (HERI)
3005 Moore Hall, Box 951521
Los Angeles, CA 90095-1521
(310) 825-1925
e-mail: heri@ucla.edu
Web site: www.gseis.ucla.edu

The Higher Education Research Institute (HERI) is an interdisciplinary center for postsecondary research, located at the University of California at Los Angeles. The insitute's research program covers a variety of topics, including the outcomes of postsecondary education, leadership development, faculty performance, federal and state policy, and educational equity. Each year HERI publishes the *American Freshman: National Norms,* as well as other specialized publications, such as the *American Freshman: 40 Year Trends* and *How Service Learning Affects Students.*

Institute of Education Sciences (IES)
U.S. Department of Education
555 New Jersey Ave. NW

Washington, DC 20208
(800) 872-53276
Web site: http://ies.ed.gov

The Institute of Education Sciences (IES) was established within the U.S. Department of Education by the Education Sciences Reform Act of 2002. IES supports rigorous, scientifically based research that is intended to improve student outcomes and the quality of education in the United States. The agency is also the primary federal provider of statistics on the condition of education at preschool, elementary, secondary, postsecondary, and adult levels, including education data from other nations.

Intercollegiate Studies Institute, Inc. (ISI)
3901 Centerville Rd., PO Box 4431
Wilmington, DE 19807-0431
(800) 526-7022
e-mail: info@isi.org
Web site: www.isi.org

The Intercollegiate Studies Institute (ISI) is a nonprofit educational organization whose purpose is to further in successive generations of college youth a better understanding of the values and institutions that sustain a free and humane society. The organization publishes several journals such as the *Intercollegiate Review, Modern Age,* a quarterly forum for conservatism's preeminent thinkers, and *the Political Science Reviewer,* an annual journal of political philosophy.

**National Association of State Universities
and Land-Grant Colleges (NASULGC)**
1307 New York Ave. NW, Ste. 400
Washington, DC 20005-4722
(202) 478-6040
Web site: www.nasulgc.org

The National Association of State Universities and Land-Grant Colleges (NASULGC) is a nonprofit association of public research universities, land-grant institutions, and many state university systems. The association's primary mission is to support high-quality public higher education and its member institutions as they perform their teaching, research, and public service roles. NASULGC publishes the online newsletter *A Public Voice* as well as many other special reports on various subjects.

National Center for Fair and Open Testing (FairTest)
15 Court Sq., Ste. 820
Boston, MA 02108
(857) 350-8207
Web site: www.fairtest.org

The National Center for Fair and Open Testing (FairTest) works to end the misuses and flaws of standardized testing and to ensure that evaluation of students, teachers, and schools is fair, open, valid, and educationally beneficial. The organization publishes the newsletter the *FairTest Examiner* as well as periodic special reports and videos on student testing.

National Center for Public Policy and Higher Education
152 North Third St., Ste. 705
San Jose, CA 95112
(408) 271-2699
e-mail: center@highereducation.org
Web site: www.highereducation.org

The National Center for Public Policy and Higher Education is a nonprofit organization that promotes public policies that enhance Americans' opportunities to pursue and achieve high-quality education and training beyond high school. The center serves as a resource for information and as a catalyst for change when needed. The center publishes the quarterly journal *National CrossTalk* as well as several series such as *Perspectives in Public Policy: Connecting Higher Education and the Public Schools*, and *Policy Alert*.

**The Pell Institute for the Study of
Opportunity in Higher Education**
1025 Vermont Ave. NW, Ste. 1020
Washington, DC 20005
(202) 638-2887
Web site: www.pellinstitute.org

The Pell Institute for the Study of Opportunity in Higher Education conducts and disseminates research and policy analysis to encourage policy makers, educators, and the public to improve educational opportunities and outcomes for low-income, first-generation, and disabled college students. The Pell Institute publishes the annual journal *Opportunity Matters* as well as many special reports, policy briefs, occasional papers, and an electronic newsletter.

For Further Reading

Books

Asher, Donald. *Cool Colleges: For the Hyper-Intelligent, Self-Directed, Late-Blooming, and Just Plain Different.* Berkley, CA: Ten Speed, 2007. The author profiles more than forty innovative and unorthodox schools and reveals best-kept secrets in higher education for outstanding and unusual students.

Attewell, Paul A., and David E. Lavin. *Passing the Torch: Does Higher Education for the Disadvantaged Pay Off Across the Generations?* New York: Russell Sage Foundation, 2007. The authors follow students admitted under the City University of New York's "open admissions" policy, tracking its effects on them and their children, to find out whether widening college access can accelerate social mobility across generations.

Bok, Derek Curtis. *Our Underachieving Colleges.* Princeton, NJ: Princeton University Press, 2006. A former Harvard president examines whether students are actually learning what they're "supposed" to learn in college.

Bowen, William G., Martin A. Kurzweil, and Eugene M. Tobin. *Equity and Excellence in American Higher Education.* Charlottesville: University of Virginia Press, 2005. The authors explore whether there is equity in college access and learning for students of all backgrounds.

Braskamp, Larry A., Larry A. Trautvetter, Lois Calian, and Kelly Ward. *Putting Students First: How Colleges Develop Students Purposefully.* Bolton, MA: Anker 2006. The authors explore the idea of holistic student development and the ways some colleges are attending to the mind, the body, and the spirit of their students.

Chace, William. *100 Semesters: My Adventures as Student, Professor, and University President, and What I Learned Along the Way.* Princeton, NJ: Princeton University Press, 2006. The author follows his own journey as a student, a teacher, and a college president to illustrate the evolution of American higher education over the last fifty years.

Golden, Daniel. *The Price of Admission: How America's Ruling Class Buys Its Way into Elite Colleges—and Who Gets Left Outside the Gates.* New

York: Crown, 2006. The author argues that America's richest families receive special access to elite higher education at the expense of those more deserving but less fortunate.

Levine, Donald Nathan. *Powers of the Mind: The Reinvention of Liberal Learning in America.* Chicago: University of Chicago Press, 2006. The author proposes methods to help revive liberal learning at American colleges and universities.

Light, Richard J. *Making the Most of College: Students Speak Their Minds.* Cambridge, MA: Harvard University Press, 2004. The author interviews hundreds of Harvard students to get their insights on how to get the most out of college.

Mathews, Jay. *Harvard Schmarvard: Getting Beyond the Ivy League to the College That Is Best for You.* New York: Three Rivers, 2003. A Harvard graduate says it does not really matter where you go to college. What is most important is within you and finding a college that fits.

Pope, Loren. *Colleges That Change Lives: 40 Schools You Should Know About Even if You're Not a Straight-A Student.* New York: Penguin, 2000. The author profiles forty small liberal arts colleges that he says can change a student's life.

Shapiro, Harold T. *A Larger Sense of Purpose: Higher Education and Society.* Princeton, NJ: Princeton University Press, 2005. A former president of Yale and the University of Michigan explores the role the modern university should play as an ethical force and societal steward.

Unger, Harlow G. *But What if I Don't Want to Go to College?* New York: Facts On File, 1998.

Vedder, Richard K. *Going Broke by Degree: Why College Costs Too Much.* Washington, DC: AEI, 2004. A college professor examines why college tuition costs so much and suggests revolutionary ways to bring college costs down.

Periodicals

Boyd, Shaun. "The True Value of a College Degree," Lifereboot.com, August 14, 2007. www.lifereboot.com/2007/the-true-value-of-a-college-degree.

Carey, Kevin. "Truth Without Action: The Myth of Higher-Education Accountability," *Change: The Magazine of Higher Learning.* September/October 2007.

Clark, Kim. "Trying to Climb a Broken Ladder," *U.S. News & World Report*, September 15, 2008.

de Vise, Daniel. "Honors Courses Give Way to AP Rigor," *Washington Post*, May 19, 2008. www.washingtonpost.com/wp-dyn/content/article/2008/05/18/AR2008051802461_pf.html.

Easterbrook, Gregg. "Who Needs Harvard?" *Atlantic Monthly*, October 2004. www.ctcl.com/pdf/Who_Needs_Harvard.pdf.

Farrell, Elizabeth F., and Martin Van Der Werf. "Playing the Rankings Game," *Chronicle of Higher Education*, May 25, 2007.

Fields, Cheryl. "Ranking Game," *Change: The Magazine of Higher Learning*, November/December, 2005.

Forbes. "Five Reasons to Skip College," April 18, 2006. www.forbes.com/2006/04/15/dont-go-college_cx_lh_06slate_0418skipcollege.html.

George, William P. "Learning Alone: Solitude and Undergraduate Education," *America*, September 15, 2008.

Hallett, Vicky. "Narrowing Your Choices," *U.S. News & World Report*, September 1, 2008.

Helm, Peyton R. "'Hearsay' Isn't the Way to Choose a College," *Morning Call Op-Ed*, June 29, 2007. www.muhlenberg.edu/mgt/presoff/essay23.html.

Hoover, Eric. "The Rankings Rainbow," *Chronicle of Higher Education*, September 2007.

Jones, Del. "Less People Choosing Ivy League," *USA Today*, April 7, 2005. www.usatoday.com/educate/college/careers/CEOs/news4-7-05.htm.

Journal of Blacks in Higher Education. "More Blacks Are Competing in Advanced Placement Programs, but the Racial Scoring Gap Is Widening," 2008. www.jbhe.com/features/59_apscoringgap.html.

Joyner, James. "Elite Schools Emphasizing SAT Scores at a Cost of Racial Diversity," *Outside the Beltway*, March 27, 2008. www.outsidethebeltway.com/archives/2008/03/elite_schools_emphasizing_sat_scores_at_cost_of_racial_diversity.

Mathews, Jay. "What to Look for in a Good School," *Washington Post*, May 20, 2003.

Menard, Valerie. "What You Know Will Help You: Antonio Flores: President and CEO, Hispanic Association of College and Universities," *Latino Leaders*, September/October 2008.

Murray, Charles. "College Daze," *Forbes*, September 1, 2008.

National Public Radio. "The College Admissions Game," February 22, 2007. www.npr.org/templates/story/story.php?storyId=7537888.

Ramirez, Eddy. "Opting Out of AP Classes," *U.S. News & World Report*, September 29, 2008.

Schmidt, Peter. "At the Elite Colleges—Dim White Kids," *Boston Globe*, September 28, 2007. www.boston.com/news/globe/editorial_opinion/oped/articles/2007/09/28/at_the_elite_colleges__dim_white_kids.

Tantillo, Astrida Orle. "Reforming College: What Professors Don't Tell You," *Slate*, November 17, 2005. www.slate.com/id/2130327.

Taylor, M.C. "The Devoted Student," *New York Times*, December 21, 2006.

Washington Monthly. "A Different Kind of College Ranking," June 2007. www2.washingtonmonthly.com/features/2007/0709.guideintro.html.

Wolfe, Alan. "College Makeover: When Ideas Kill," *Slate*, November 15, 2005. www.slate.com/id/2130322.

Index

College Board, 41, 122, 130
College campuses, drinking on, 7–10
College completion rates, 32
College costs. *See* Costs
College endowments, *63*
College graduates
  children of, 16
  earnings of, 13, *14,* 101
  productivity of, 89, 90
College preparation
  defining adequate, 30–39
  high schools are lacking in, 24–29
College professors
  at small liberal arts colleges, 76–78
  suspicion of, 100
  teaching skills of, 38
  tenure for, 93
College rankings
  factors in, *57*
  flaws in, 59–64
  helpfulness of, 54–58
College readiness, defining, 30–39
College selection process
  real-world experiences and, 65–69
  U.S. News & World Report rankings and, 54–64
College students
  binge drinking by, 7–10
  boomerang, 66–67, *68*
  disinterested, 19–20
  low-income, 114–120
  minority, 38
  substance abuse among, *21*
College(s)
  attendance patterns, 15–16
  benefits of, 12–17
  as commodity, 101
  is not for everyone, 18–23
  Ivy League, 70–73
  liberal arts, 74–80, 102–103
  See also Universities
Colorado State University (CSU), 7
Computers, 34
Conley, David T., 35–36
Core curriculum, in high school, 25–29, 31
Costs
  of college are too high, 87–97
  at public universities, 83, 84
  reasons for rising, 92–96, 98–106
Critical thinking skills, 35

D
Deaths, alcohol-related, 7–8
Diver, Colin, 102
Dodd, Barbara, 43, 44
Drinking, on college campuses, 7–10
Drinking age, 7–10
Drunk driving, 9
Dual enrollment, 45–46

E
Earnings, of college vs. high school graduates, *14,* 89, 101
Economic rent, 94

Price discrimination, 94,
100
Public universities
admissions to, 85
advantages of, 81
costs at, 83, *84*
disadvantages of, 84

R
Real-world experiences,
65–69
Reed College, 105–106
Remedial courses, 36–37
Research grants, 94
Ruecker, Ronald, 9

S
SAT II, 130
SAT tests
average scores of, *124*
percentage of students
who take, *130*
should be eliminated,
121–126
should not be eliminated,
127–131
writing section of,
130–131
Schmeiser, Cyndie, 34
Shulman, Sam, 76
Skills
needed for college success,
35–38
writing, 128–131
Small colleges
advantages of, 74–80
costs at, 102–103

Societal benefits, of higher
education, 14–15
Socioeconomic background
acceptance rates and, 123–125
postsecondary participation
patterns and, 15
of students at wealthy
institutions, 113–120
Spady, Samantha, 7, 10, *11*
Spence, David S., 34
St. Lawrence University,
115–117
Standardized tests
should be eliminated,
121–126
should not be eliminated,
127–131
Standards for Success, 35
Standards movement, 32
Stanford University, *56*
Stanley-Becker, Tom, 48
Stone, Marvin L., 55
Substance abuse, *21*
Sullivan, Daniel F., 112
Swanson, Mary Catherine, 38

T
Tenure, 93
Test scores, 114–115
See also Admissions tests
Third party payments, 92
Tobin, Eugene M., 114
Toomey, Michael, 18
Tuition
costs are too high, 87–97
at public universities, 83, *84*
reasons for high, 98–106

Picture Credits

© Angela Hampton Picture Library/Alamy, 37

AP Images, 11, 102

Christopher Barth/Newhouse News Service/Landov, 53

© Richard Cummins/SuperStock, 56

Image copyright GWImages, 2008. Used under license from Shutterstock.com, 109

© Jan Halaska/Alamy, 61

John Nordell/*The Christian Science Monitor* via Getty Images, 123

© Nancy Palmieri/Bloomberg News/Landov, 77

Bob Pearson/AFP/Getty Images, 129

Fred Prouser/Reuters/Landov, 91

Bill Pugliano/Getty Images, 82

Lara Jo Regan/Liaison/Getty Images, 42, 49

Mario Ruiz/Time Life Pictures/Getty Images, 86

© The Stock Asylum, LLC/Alamy, 16

© William Strode/SuperStock, 67

© SuperStock/Inc./SuperStock, 71

Essdras M. Suarez/Boston Globe/Landov, 114

© ThinkStock/SuperStock, 28